CHAIRMAN OR CHIEF?

— the role of Taoiseach in Irish Government

Studies in Irish Political Culture 1

CHAIRMAN OR CHIEF?

—the role of Taoiseach in Irish Government

BRIAN FARRELL

GILL AND MACMILLAN

Published by
GILL AND MACMILLAN LTD
2 Belvedere Place
Dublin 1

and in London through association with the
MACMILLAN
Group of Publishing Companies

7171 0535 0

Cover designed by Graham Shepherd

Printing history:
10 9 8 7 6 5 4 3 2 1

Printed and bound in the Republic of Ireland by
CAHILL & CO. LIMITED DUBLIN 8

Contents

Preface

The rapid growth of numbers in senior schools, techno-
logical colleges and universities has been accompanied by a
growing interest in how Irish society is governed. Students of
law, history, economics and sociology, as well as those directly
involved in political science and public administration are
questioning the methods, institutions, and values of contemporary politics. They are concerned to relate their own,
perhaps very limited, experiences of Irish political behaviour
to the professed ideals often presented to them. That concern
is shared by many other citizens.

The purpose of this series is to help in these enquiries. It
attempts to provide basic tools of analysis and organised
sources of information by examining various approaches to
central themes in the contemporary study of political institutions, philosophy and behaviour. Certain titles in the series
are presented as edited readers, bringing together previously
published but scattered treatments of particular topics, others
are extended essays on significant problems. The intention is
to combine the most recent research findings, detailed data
and case-studies with broad-based generalisations and appli-
cations.

The general title, *Studies in Irish Political Culture,* is
deliberately chosen to indicate that the series will not be
limited by any narrowly institutional or purely governmental
emphasis. Political culture embraces the spirit as well as the
form of public institutions and laws, the traditions of a society
and its historical experience, the behaviour and values of
élites and of the mass of citizens. The series is planned to
avoid any single, static analytic design and to recruit the
assistance of workers in many disciplines in order to reach a
new understanding of how modern Irish society sees, governs
and directs its affairs.

Introduction: The Modern Executive

Executive power is at the heart of modern government. There was a brief period in the nineteenth century, between the collapse of the old absolutist kingdoms and empires of the *ancien régime* and the rise of the modern state machine, when it seemed otherwise. In the years between the two great Reform Bills of 1832 and 1867 British parliamentary sovereignty offered a new model of representative government. Woodrow Wilson, as an academic political scientist, was ready to substitute the British parliamentary model for the American presidential system. At that time, governmental functions were largely limited to the maintenance of internal order and stability and to defence of the state against external enemies. Kings were losing their crowns and prerogatives; the power of the executive was in decline.

The rapid extension of governmental responsibility and activity in the twentieth century has reversed that trend. Now, the central role of the executive is visible and acknowledged. All modern states are 'welfare states', accepting responsibility for a wide range of services not only for under-privileged minorities but for the great mass of citizens; all are, to some extent, involved in engineering economic growth and planning. The demands made on the state and the duties accepted by it are constantly expanding—from roads, education, medical services into scientific research, the environment, sports, the arts. The growth is reflected in large bureaucratic machines and in the tendency for the state to consume an ever-larger share of the gross national product. It is accompanied by an emphasis on planning: proper allocation of scarce resources demands that decisions in a variety of areas interlock, that priorities are clearly established and costed, and that the overall direction of policy is clear. This, in turn, has led to a concentration of power and influence within the executive. The head of government has become the visible symbol of state authority; the demand for political leadership incessant.

In some systems this has led to the creation of autocracies and dictatorships. In almost all political systems, executive dominance and the personification of this domination in a single leader is a central fact of political life. The development occurs conspicuously and dramatically in new states: Castro becomes synonymous with Cuba, Nkrumah with Ghana, Nasser with modern Egypt. It is evident in the most established and stable countries: a post-war British prime minister becomes 'Macwonder', the figure of 'der Alte' straddles the opening decades of Federal West Germany, France invokes de Gaulle in order to suspend divisive conflict and avert social disintegration. For all the growing size, intensity and complexity of the modern governmental machine, there is still a continuous process of power concentration, a pyramid of decision-making, at the apex of which is a single man. In Harry Truman's incisive phrase 'the buck stops here'. Erwin C. Hargrove has commented:

> political scientists write of the inevitability of the 'personalisation of power' in modern industrial society. It is suggested that as the old politics of class and ideological conflict decline in Europe, as television becomes the chief means of political information for the public, as parties and parliaments weaken before the executive, power will increasingly become visible to people through popular leaders and these leaders will be the chief means of engaging the political interest of publics.[1]

The modern leader has a complex role to play. He is chief executive, commonly also party leader, invariably in effect principal legislator, national spokesman, main ideologist, available scapegoat. And he is required to play all these roles, perform all these functions simultaneously and in the glare of an inescapable publicity.[2] The rules and circumstances vary. In a presidential system, in theory at least, the concept of the separation of powers may weaken his control of the assembly—it is certainly likely to make greater demands on his stock of political resources; in a parliamentary system, he may appear to be bound by notions of answerability and of collective responsibility.

There is no single rule for the selection of political leaders, no one avenue by which they attain power, no one standard by which to judge their capacity. The man's own personality, experience and ambition to govern will affect his performance. 'Some leaders are shepherds, some are wolves, and some fit neither metaphor.'[3] Max Weber adopted a three-fold analysis of leadership based on the sources of authority, which has been subjected to some severe criticism in recent years.[4] A simpler analysis suggests that modern heads of government fall into two main categories—the chiefs and the chairmen. The particular circumstances of the leader, the character of the political system, and the style of authority within the society are all appropriate dimensions of this typology. The 'chief' is distinguished by a tendency to accumulate political resources, concentrate decision-making and, above all, make use of his position to mobilise the machinery of government for action; the 'chairman' is prepared to allow others to share both resources and responsibility and prone to value the maintenance of existing procedures. The 'chief' corresponds to the type identified by Bertrand de Jouvenal as 'dux' and by Sidney Hook, among others, as 'hero'—he is dynamic, an activist and a promoter of action.[5] The 'chairman' is closer to Weber's model of 'rational-legal authority'—he acquires office through an established procedure and seeks no more than the authority of that institutional office to implement policy; he is a routine leader, more conscious of methods than of goals. The distinction has been summarised by Stanley Hoffmann :

the heroic leader seizes responsibility as a sword instead of hiding behind the shield of committee procedures; he deliberately puts the spotlight on his acts and claims personal authorship even for measures actually instituted below him . . . The heroic leader tends to thirst for responsibility, just as the routine leader longs for absolution.[6]

Particular systems favour one or other type of leadership; particular circumstances and time periods appear to invoke the same type of leadership in totally different systems.

This essay attempts to interpret the role of head of government in Ireland since the foundation of the state and to examine briefly the performance of its successive incumbents with particular reference to their cabinet relations. It takes as its starting-point the current discussion in Britain on the role of the Prime Minister; describes the constitutional, legal and administrative position of the office of Taoiseach; surveys broadly the relationship of Taoiseach and cabinet under Cosgrave, de Valera, Costello, Lemass, concluding with a tentative assessment of the office under the present Taoiseach; finally, it poses the question: to what extent does the office require a chairman or a chief?

It would not have been possible without the help, co-operation and confidence of a large number of current and former ministers, deputies, senators, senior civil servants, academic and journalistic colleagues. I am especially indebted to some of the most senior of modern Irish statesmen, including three Taoisigh and five other major party leaders, for their willingness to be interviewed and consulted. While this work would not have been possible and while it must certainly have been far less accurate as a representation of the role of Taoiseach, without this and other assistance which cannot be acknowledged here, the present author alone is responsible for the following interpretation of the office and account of its various incumbents.

NOTES: Introduction

[1]Erwin C. Hargrove, 'Political Leadership in the Anglo-American Democracies', in *Political Leadership in Industrialised Societies: studies in comparative analysis,* ed. Lewis J. Edinger, New York 1967, 182.

[2]This point is registered forcefully in Richard E. Neustadt, *Presidential Power: the politics of leadership*, New York 1962, preface viii.

[3]James C. Davies, *Human Nature in Politics*, New York 1963, 278.

[4]Max Weber, *The Theory of Social and Economic Organisation*, New York 1964, 359-392. For two critical examinations of Weber's typology see Carl J. Friedrich, 'Political Leadership and the Problem of Charismatic Power', *Journal of Politics*, XXIII, 1 (February 1961) and K. J. Ratnam, 'Charisma and Political Leadership', *Political Studies*, XII, 3 (March 1963).

[5]Bertrand de Jouvenal, *Sovereignty*. Sidney Hook, *The Hero in History*, Boston 1943. Cf. Athur M. Schlesinger Jr., *The Politics of Hope*, London 1964.

[6]Stanley Hoffman, 'Heroic Leadership: the case of modern France', in *Political Leadership in Industrialised Societies*, 132.

xiii

1

The Office

The close resemblance between the Irish system of government and the British cabinet model from which it derives is well established. Rather less attention has been paid to the fact that the model was already obsolete when it was adopted. Bagehot and other nineteenth century writers may well have identified the elements of representative control of the executive operative between the Reform Bills of 1832 and 1867. But by the end of the first World War the hegemony of the cabinet within the system was well established. Since then, and more particularly since the end of the second World War, 'it has become part of the conventional wisdom expressed by some academics and journalists that the position of the Prime Minister in the British system of government has altered significantly'; he has become the 'focal point of modern cabinets'; there has been a 'trend towards greater concentration of power and authority in the Prime Minister'.[1] It has become possible to speak of Britain moving from a parliamentary to a presidential system with the Prime Minister acting out the role of real executive head.

A number of factors have contributed to the change: the very considerable increase in the range, powers and size of government; the growing professionalism of politics; the channelling of information to the centre; the growing emphasis on the personality of the party leaders, stimulated both by the mass media and by the application of modern advertising and public relations techniques to political campaigns; the recognition that the generalised image of the party (in large measure moulded round the *persona* of the leader) is more important in gaining electoral support than either specific issues or individual candidates in constituencies.

1

The debate is less one of fact than of emphasis. The modern Prime Minister is immeasurably more powerful than his cabinet-bound predecessor of the last century. But to what extent do the traditional constraints of collective responsibility and conventions of parliamentary answerability still obtain? If the question can be asked of a post-war selection of British leaders that includes Home and Eden as well as Churchill, Attlee and Macmillan, it seems even more pertinent in the context of Irish political leadership with the development of the cabinet crisis in May 1970.

In any governmental system the number of men who reach the top is small; in Ireland literally only a handful of men have led government since the adoption of the Irish Free State Constitution in 1922. These five (Cosgrave, de Valera, Costello, Lemass, Lynch) compare with nine Presidents of the United States and twelve British Prime Ministers in the same period of time. This concentration of leadership might well lead one to suppose that in Ireland the cabinet form of collective responsibility must by now have given way to a more 'presidential' distillation of executive power. Initial observations appear to confirm that view.

For the best part of forty years after the foundation of the state de Valera dominated Irish politics. His *charisma* was recognised by political opponents as well as by intensely loyal supporters. In 1933, speaking on the motion nominating the President of the Executive Council, Frank MacDermott said:

> the personality of the President is capable of being a great asset to this country. I disagree with almost everything he has done in public life, but I recognise the hold which he has obtained over the imagination and the affections of a large proportion of our people, and, particularly, our young people. (*Dáil Debates* 46/21, 8 February 1933.)

Foreign and domestic observers alike have paid their tributes. 'An English historian claimed that in many respects he was the most remarkable figure in post-Versailles Europe ... some measure of his impact is provided by the steady interest he

2

aroused outside Ireland'; Professor Chubb wrote of de Valera's last general election campaign: 'owing to his unique position in the country's history, his ability and his enormous personal following in the country, the party has always revolved around "the Chief" '; typically a French author has commented: 'le long *règne* de de Valera a créé une tradition de *leadership* énergique et de grande popularité personelle qui faisait du Premier ministre l'élu de la nation.'[2]

Clearly the role of head of government must inevitably be affected by the performance of a man who has held office for twenty-one years, sixteen of them continuously. Yet it is also evident that the man himself will be influenced and shaped by the conventions and traditions of the post. The reiterated emphasis on de Valera's personality has tended to distort an understanding of his leadership style and to obscure the institutional role of the Taoiseach in the Irish system.

The electoral appeal of the party leader in Ireland is moderated by the exigencies of proportional representation and by the intensely local perspective of Irish politics. The fact that two out of every three Dáil deputies were born in the constituency they represent and three out of four live in their own electoral area underlines the potential independence of local party organisations, and their representatives, from centralised control and discipline. The virtual impossibility of imposing candidates successfully on a local list is a further reflection of this local autonomy and represents a distinct limitation on the leader's influence and patronage. Nevertheless, the leader is the main standard-bearer of the party's fortunes and among party leaders, an incumbent Taoiseach has a pre-eminent position. It is his position, not his personality, which puts him into the centre of the electoral stage. The fact is evident in the three general elections since de Valera relinquished office—elections in which the voters were exhorted initially to 'let Lemass lead on' and subsequently urged 'Let's back Jack'. In Ireland, as in Britain, general elections have acquired some of the characteristics of a plebiscite, a political popularity contest, in which the party images are personalised through the leaders. Campaigns are built around extensive tours of the countryside. Both commentators and partisans accept, for instance, that in the 1969 election it was Mr. Lynch's own efforts that countered an anti-government trend. The question is : to what extent does this electoral influence reflect the strength of the leader in office?

In Ireland, the head of government's powers do not merely derive from political conventions. They are defined constitutionally and limited by legislative provisions. Under the original Dáil Constitution of 1919 the head of government was rather ambiguously termed 'President'. This usage seems to have been adopted during de Valera's tour of the United States in this period; for an American audience the title carried more significance than the more conventional term 'Prime Minister.' There is the further point that the Dáil Constitution made no provision for a head of state; it did not even define the character of the new regime. The true status of head of government was more accurately expressed in the Irish title 'Priomh-Aire'; he was 'first minister', parliament's elected leader and the man who nominated its ministers. It is now clear that in drafting the Irish Free State Constitution three years later, a conscious effort was made to break completely with the conventions of the British party system. Although the Committee which drafted the original proposals differed more sharply on the form of the executive to be adopted than on any other issue, there was evident a common desire to contain and control executive power.[3] In line with the trend of constitutional thinking in the twenties, the main emphasis was on popular participation (through the referendum and initiative) and direct representation of interests. The draft constitution initially accepted by the Provisional Government required the appointment, by an impartial Dáil committee, of 'extern' ministers. These expert 'extern' administrative heads of department were to be allocated on a functional basis; they might be chosen from the whole body of citizens and would hold office for the full life of a Dáil unless removed from office for malfeasance, incompetence or failure to carry out the expressed will of the House. During the debate on the

4

constitution in the Constituent Assembly this provision was modified to permit such 'extern' ministers to be appointed as an optional aid to government. Very few men were in fact appointed in this experimental blend of British and Swiss practice and all were party men. The scheme was abandoned in 1927.

The thrust of the Irish Free State Constitution was not designed to encourage any large-scale growth in the powers of the governmental head (now termed 'President of the Executive Council'). He was required to submit the names of his cabinet to the Dáil for approval; the minimum and maximum numbers were specified and he was required to retire from office should he fail to retain majority support in the Dáil; the power of dissolution was vested in the Executive Council as a whole and a defeated cabinet was specifically debarred from demanding a dissolution. The effect of these limitations, as Professor Mansergh pointed out, was 'to deprive the head of the Council of those powers which *par excellence* distinguish his position from that of his colleagues'.[4] Although in fact circumstances pushed the Irish Free State to abandon the 'Swiss' features of the Constitution in favour of the British cabinet model, they could not entirely erode the built-in safeguards against executive concentration. The President of the Executive Council was destined to be chairman of his cabinet, not its master.

The 1937 Constitution altered that relationship. Indeed in the course of the Dáil debate on the Constitution it was constantly asserted by Opposition speakers that both the new office of President of Ireland and that of Taoiseach represented a dangerous concentration of power. The comparisons made between the old office of President of the Executive Council and the new office of Taoiseach are indicative of existing attitudes among senior politicians. Thus J. A. Costello, a former Attorney-General destined to become Taoiseach eleven years later, argued:

Under the existing Constitution the President of the Executive Council is merely a member of the Executive

5

Council. The Executive Council is the Government of this State with collective responsibility and each and every Minister has a dignity and responsibility. Preserved here in the new Constitution . . . is the semblance of collective responsibility . . . analysed it means that the Prime Minister has control over each and every one of the members of the Government. He can dismiss them . . . it takes only the Prime Minister at his will and pleasure, without a meeting of the Executive Council, without coming to the Dáil, whose servant he is supposed to be.

(*Dáil Debates* 67/301-2, 12 May 1937.)

Patrick McGilligan, a former Minister for Industry and Commerce and future Minister for Finance and Attorney-General, also argued that the dismissal of ministers should remain a function of the government as a whole, and William Norton, leader of the Labour Party, objected to a constitutional proposal that would give the head of government 'unreasonably wide powers'. (*Dáil Debates* 67/1301 and 1173, 26 May 1937.)

In the event, despite these and other objections, the Constitution was adopted. Unambiguously it lays down that the Taoiseach is 'Head of Government'. Some powers are performed by the President as head of state but only on the advice of the Taoiseach. Thus the President appoints the members of the government, but on the nomination of the Taoiseach and with the approval of the Dáil. It is the Taoiseach who allocates ministers to departments and who can demand their resignation. The Taoiseach retains the right of dissolution, which can only be denied to a Taoiseach who has lost the confidence of a majority in the Dáil; he nominates the Attorney-General and also eleven members of the Senate. His position as head of government is further illustrated by the provision that if at any time he resigns from office, the other members of government are deemed to have resigned with him. It was the clear intention of de Valera in framing these provisions to redress the balance of the Irish Free State Constitution, which had reduced the role of the

President of the Executive Council, and to elevate the office of Taoiseach to a level comparable in status to that of the modern British Prime Minister.

The constitutional positioning of the Taoiseach at the centre of the stage is reinforced in administrative practice. Seán Lemass has defined the office in these terms: 'the main function of the Taoiseach is to facilitate the taking of decisions by the Government'.[5] It is in this administrative definition of the post that the unbroken continuity of head of government office, whether termed 'President of the Executive Council' or 'Taoiseach', is best exemplified. His department, from the outset, has been the cabinet office; his officials, servants of the government as a whole. Arguably, this has been a factor of some significance in containing any extension of prime ministerial power. Certainly one former Secretary of the Department of the Taoiseach, Muiris Ó Muimhneacháin, has emphasised in some detail this managerial role of the Taoiseach as 'the captain of the team':

he is the central co-ordinating figure who takes an interest in the work of all departments, the figure to whom ministers naturally turn for advice and guidance when faced with problems involving large questions of policy or otherwise of special difficulty and whose leadership is essential to the successful working of the government as a collective authority, collectively responsible to Dáil Éireann, but acting through members, each of whom is charged with specific departmental tasks. He may often have to inform himself in considerable detail of particular matters with which other members of the government are primarily concerned. He may have to make public statements on such matters as well as on general matters of broad policy, internal and external. He answers Dáil Questions where the attitude of the government towards important matters of policy is involved. He may occasionally sponsor Bills which represent new developments of policy, even when the legislation when enacted, will be the particular concern of the minister in charge of some other department

7

of state. His department is the sole channel of communication between departments generally and the President's secretariat, except in minor and routine matters. Through his parliamentary secretary, whose office is also included in the department of the Taoiseach, he secures the coordination, in a comprehensive parliamentary programme, of the proposals of the various ministers for legislative and other measures in the Houses of the Oireachtas.[6]

However neither constitutional provision nor administrative arrangements can fully represent the dynamics of the office. In the mid-twenties Asquith commented 'the office of Prime Minister is what its holder chooses and is able to make of it'.[7] In the *Léargas* interview already quoted Lemass expressed the view that 'it would not be possible to define the role of the Taoiseach in a precise way which would be applicable to all men in all circumstances'. More formally, the Devlin Report on the organisation of the Irish public service recorded the judgement 'different Taoiseachs will have different requirements'. They will bring their own policy concerns and preferences to the office; they will enlist new supports, acquire new debts, recruit new men, confront new political situations. Nevertheless, after fifty years of self-government, it should be possible to define in some broad outline at least the central question of the relationship of Taoiseach and cabinet as it has developed in Ireland. There are no easy answers since none of the major actors have yet published comprehensive memoirs. We are dependent on Dáil and Senate debates, newspaper articles and personal observations, conversations and a series of interviews for data. These data must obviously be incomplete and provisional but the effort to supply some form of institutional analysis must be made. The enquiry might be posed in terms borrowed from the British debate on prime ministerial power: is the Taoiseach *primus inter pares* or, behind the dignified facade of the cabinet government model, do we uncover the really efficient secret of prime ministerial power?

In Britain much of the debate has concentrated on a few

dramatic cases of ministerial sackings—more especially Macmillan's purge of seven members of his cabinet, including the Chancellor of the Exchequer, in July 1962. Just as important, of course, in assessing the relationship are initial appointments, subsequent promotions and demotions and resignations.

The Irish political system is much smaller and more intimate than the British. This might be seen as offering even greater possibilities for parliamentary patronage, a significant factor in developing the political influence of the British Prime Minister. The danger was noted by Bryan Cooper, T.D., speaking on the Ministers and Secretaries Bill :

> you are going to take nineteen salaried ministers out of an Assembly that is only one hundred strong, and if we anticipate, as we may, that the dominant party will naturally and rightly select these ministers from their own party, you are going to take nineteen paid officials out of a party of little more than sixty. . . . By this Bill it is proposed to have one-third of the dominant party in receipt of salaries or holding office.
>
> (*Dáil Debates* 5/947, 16 November 1923.)

In practice, the small scale has had the effect of severely limiting the number of deputies available to any Taoiseach for appointment; it has been a curb on his power rather than an enhancement of his patronage. The problem was mentioned, with rather more accurate figures than Cooper offered, in the all-party interim *Report of the Committee on the Constitution*.

> On the basis of present Dáil membership, the deputies supporting the government are likely to number seventy or so. As many of these would for one good reason or another be unable to take up ministerial office, the Taoiseach is, in effect, left with some thirty-five or forty deputies out of whom he must find about twenty ministers and parliamentary secretaries.

9

Two holders of the office of Taoiseach, when asked by the present writer about the selection of members for appointment, immediately spoke about this difficulty of filling twenty offices from such a small number of deputies. Clearly the scale of Irish politics, and perhaps a continuing part-time emphasis among deputies, imposes a limitation of choice of which any Taoiseach will be conscious. It is known that at least one Dublin Fianna Fáil back-bencher refused an offer of office, initially as parliamentary secretary and subsequently as Minister, because of business commitments in the mid-sixties; he did not offer himself for selection as a Dáil candidate in 1969. This reluctance of some deputies means that those who are prepared to be fulltime politicians and take office (especially if they have any degree of seniority in the party, or personal support, or a firm economic independence) may lay down some conditions with regard to what positions they are prepared to accept. So it appears that the small scale of Irish politics represents a curb on the patronage and power of the Taoiseach.

It has also been suggested on occasions that regional considerations affect the composition of cabinets and choice of ministers. This is indeed a feature of government formation in many systems—noticeably the American cabinet and to a lesser extent British Labour administrations. An examination of the Irish experience indicates that this is not a major consideration. Speaking in the Dáil in 1964, Lemass made the point that only three of the fourteen ministers sat for Dublin constituencies and commented :

> I do not think it can be contended that Dublin city is over-represented in the government, although, in my view, it is the qualifications and experience of individual deputies which should operate in the mind of a Taoiseach when choosing any deputy for ministerial office.
>
> (*Dáil Debates* 212/101-2, 3 November 1964.)

In his last cabinet, Lemass was clearly not inhibited by geographical considerations. Two of the three Dublin ministers represented the same constituency and both Donegal and

Mayo were given two ministers each; only two ministers were appointed from the whole of Munster, both of them representing urban constituencies.

Another problem in clarifying the precise relationship of Taoiseach and cabinet is the lack of any clear-cut hierarchy of ministers in the Irish system. Apart from the primacy of the Taoiseach, and the special status of the Tánaiste, the only departmental minister whose rank is formally conceded is Finance. All three are required to be chosen from the Dáil and if the Tánaiste acts, according to the Constitution, 'for and in the place of the Taoiseach during the temporary absence of the Taoiseach', the Minister for Finance acts with and close to the Taoiseach at all times. They share the same accounting officer departmentally and share responsibility for the whole civil service. This follows the British pattern, linking Prime Minister and Treasury, and is a common feature of most modern executives. No other government officer can compare in power and influence with the Minister for Finance. Despite his title, the Tánaiste has no automatic right of succession; the title is a mark of seniority rather than of favour, although it may well be that a Taoiseach is more likely to consult the Tánaiste than other ministers on politically delicate matters. In the two Inter-Party governments the office of Tánaiste was used to acknowledge formally the position of William Norton as leader of the second largest party in government.

In many systems the portfolios of Foreign and of Home Affairs would be regarded as senior in the governmental hierarchy. In Ireland, although senior men have customarily held External Affairs, and that department has maintained a tradition of separate cadet recruitment from the general administrative branch of the civil service, it cannot be regarded as a key ministry in the hierarchy. Relations with Britain have always constituted the most significant element in Irish foreign policy and at all critical stages the Taoiseach himself has taken charge. In 1937 de Valera argued in the Dáil that the fact that he had retained the portfolio since 1932 was 'proof of the importance of the department from the point of view of the estimation of the government'; in 1941 he went even further to assert 'it is almost essential, in all small states, that the head of government should also be Minister for External Affairs.' (*Dáil Debates* 67/792, 19 May 1937; 102/1035, 1941). One of his closest party supporters has stressed the considerable extent to which, under de Valera, the Department of External Affairs rather than the Taoiseach's office was the centre of administrative effort; it is indicative that the work of drafting the 1937 Constitution was given to the legal adviser of that department. However, when Lemass began his exploratory talks with Captain O'Neill on Northern affairs he virtually ignored Iveagh House. Moreover in detailed negotiations on agriculture and other trading interests appropriate departments have intervened. It was further noticeable in recent years that, as the centre of Irish overseas interest shifted from the United Nations to the European Economic Community, a long-serving and influential minister, Frank Aiken, offered no resistance when responsibility was effectively transferred from his department to that of Finance. He justified his position in the Dáil:

Fianna Fáil have evolved a very strong system of collective responsibility as well as the division of administration. The Taoiseach is and has been, as is right and natural, in charge of major constitutional matters such as joining the E.E.C.   (*Dáil Debates* 201/1075.)

It is clear that in the Irish system a cachet still attaches to the External Affairs portfolio; it is an office of high prestige. It is yet to be shown as a substantial administrative power base for a potential Taoiseach.

An even more disquieting development is evident in the Home Affairs area. The Department of Justice, in the early years of the state, was regarded as a senior and sensitive responsibility. Internal security is always a serious matter, especially for new states and more particularly when a substantial minority deny the legitimacy of the regime. Although the extent of that problem has declined in Ireland over the

12

decades it remains serious. All the more curious, then, to note the pattern of appointments to the Department of Justice since 1961. Four ministers have been appointed. For three (Haughey, Lenihan, D. O'Malley) this was their first ministerial appointment, while the fourth (Ó Moráin) was only moved to Justice after nine years in the acknowledged low-status Department of Lands. Clearly, then, Justice must be regarded as a junior ministry in the Irish hierarchy.

For the rest, the two economic Departments of Industry and Commerce and of Agriculture are clearly reserved for senior, and competent, men; although the former department has lost some of its influence with the introduction of free trade policies and with the hiving-off of major functions into separate departments (Transport and Power, and Labour) and semi-state bodies. At the other end of the scale, both Lands and Defence are considered to lack political prestige, and the Gaeltacht has become a secondary concern of ministers holding other portfolios.

However, with these still-undefined exceptions there is no institutional pecking-order within the Irish ministerial hierarchy. To date it has been the man rather than his governmental office which has formed the claim to status and influence. Indeed it is a noticeable feature of Irish experience that heads of government have not risen through the ministerial ranks. Cosgrave moved straight from Local Government; de Valera's first ministerial experience was as leader; Costello had never been a member of government, although he had served as Attorney-General, before becoming Taoiseach; Lemass had stayed for twenty-one years in the one Department of Industry and Commerce, apart from a war-time sojourn in the temporary Department of Supplies; Lynch alone among Irish government leaders has served a full apprenticeship from parliamentary secretaryship through the Departments of Education, Industry and Commerce, and Finance, to the top. But to date the lack of a hierarchy has made it difficult to distinguish whether cabinet changes represented promotion, demotion or simply a response to a particular problem.

13

Another factor affecting any effort to investigate the relationship between Taoiseach and cabinet is the political longevity of the first generation of political leaders. Four of the nine men chosen to form the de Valera cabinet in 1932 were still holding office when he resigned as Taoiseach in 1959; one, Aiken, continued to serve under both Lemass and Lynch until 1969. When Fine Gael joined the first Inter-Party government in 1948, after sixteen years in opposition, they brought with them into the cabinet not only a former Attorney-General but two former members of the Executive Council.

So, we start with a governmental system which is small, in which the ranking of ministers is by seniority of service, and which until very recently has been dominated by a single generation of political leaders. These factors have certainly limited the freedom of action available to any head of government in appointing, promoting, demoting or dismissing ministers. A further limitation has been the provision of the Ministers and Secretaries Act (1924) making the appointment of parliamentary secretaries a function of the government as a whole. The Act leaves nomination to the head of government and the realities of power suggest that he will normally have the greatest say in the choice of personnel. But he will also be limited by the expectations of existing parliamentary secretaries, the wishes of senior ministers and the ambitions of powerful men in his party. It is accepted that in some cases the Taoiseach has been unable to impose junior nominees on cabinet colleagues. This may have been a consideration affecting Lemass when he deviated from convention in this matter. Both in 1961 and in 1965, when announcing the names of the new government, he went on to say: 'the appointment of parliamentary secretaries is a function of the government. I intend, when the government has been constituted, to ask them to appoint forthwith. . . .' In effect, by stating his intention Lemass was actually making the appointments, and incidentally grooming the new men for future higher office. In 1961 two of the three (D. B. O'Malley, Lenihan) were new appointments, the third (J.

14

Brennan) had been nominated by Lemass on the promotion of Gerard Bartley to be minister for the Gaeltacht on 23 July 1959. All three parliamentary secretaries became ministers before Lemass resigned in 1966; in 1965, all six parliamentary secretaries were new appointments, five of whom have since become ministers. In 1961, it is known that Lemass had already consulted some of his colleagues; in 1965 the nominations were offered without prior governmental consultation although appointments were discussed with individual ministers.

However, even this innovation could not release the parliamentary secretaries from their institutional dependence on their departmental ministers. Lemass might wish to encourage them and give them their heads but the parliamentary secretary lives in an administrative limbo and an uncooperative minister can keep him from the paradise of policy-making indefinitely. Nevertheless the nominations suggest an interesting attempt to experiment with the role of executive leadership and to assert some more dominant position for the Taoiseach *vis-à-vis* his cabinet. It might be noted that when Lynch was forming his administration following the 1969 general election it was said that he was prevailed upon by senior colleagues not to proceed with some nominations of parliamentary secretaries; the same nominees were subsequently appointed in the major re-shuffle following the government crisis of 1970. Future choices of junior appointments by a Taoiseach may be less subject to any cabinet veto.

If legislation curbs the power of a Taoiseach in regard to parliamentary secretaries, it is noticeable that no head of government has been ready to experiment with his constitutional right to appoint men directly to the Senate and nominate them to the cabinet from that House. The only such appointment ever made followed the defeat of a senior Fianna Fáil minister—Seán Moylan—in the general election of 1957. He had campaigned vigorously throughout the country and de Valera retained his services; announcing the names of his new cabinet, he stated his intention to nominate Moylan to the Senate and then to allocate to him the Department of

Education. The only other member of the Senate ever included in government was Senator Joseph Connolly who served from 1932 until the abolition of the second chamber in 1936. Three factors might be mentioned to explain why Taoisigh have failed to use their power to nominate two ministers from the Senate—a noticeable omission given their right to select eleven members of the Senate directly. First, the subservient position always accorded to the Senate; throughout Irish political development the Dáil had been the dominant legislative House. Second, a firmly entrenched reluctance to appoint men who could not claim some popular electoral mandate; this was evident in the Opposition reaction to the Moylan appointment. Third, the procedural clumsiness involved in naming a man who cannot in fact take up office until three months later (because of the delay in the actual formation of the two Houses) and who, in the Senate, is likely to become regarded as a general spokesman for the government.

This reluctance to make use af a constitutional power parallels the failure, under the Irish Free State Constitution, to use the device of 'extern' ministers to recruit talent from outside the Oireachtas. Of course, Cosgrave's inactivity in this regard might be related to the generally accepted picture of him as a colourless and unimpressive President of the Executive Council, placed beside the dominating figure of de Valera. Dr. Donal O'Sullivan has suggested that in the company of O'Higgins, Mulcahy, Hogan, O'Sullivan, McGilligan—'all highly educated men with their feet firmly on the ground . . . all of strong, in some cases, even dominant, personality'—Cosgrave 'was never more than a leader among equals.' But this image of a decent but rather ineffective leader must be modified by any objective re-appraisal of Cosgrave in office.

NOTES: The Office

[1]Quotations from G. W. Jones, 'The Prime Minister's Power', *Parliamentary Affairs*, xviii (Spring 1965), 167; John P. Mackintosh, *The British Cabinet,* 2nd ed. London 1968, 428; D. J. Heasman, 'The Prime

Minister and the Cabinet' in *The British Prime Minister: a reader,* ed. Anthony King, London 1969, 55.

[2]Quotations from T. D. Williams, 'De Valera in Power' in *The Years of the Great Test,* ed. F. MacManus, Cork 1967, 30; Basil Chubb, 'Ireland 1957' in *Elections Abroad,* ed. D. E. Butler, London 1959, 189; Georges Langrod et M. Clifford-Vaughan, *L'Irlande,* Paris 1968, 238. For similar expressions see T. P. Coogan, *Ireland Since the Rising,* London 1966, 71ff.

[3]For an account of the drafting of the Irish Free State Constitution see Brian Farrell, *The Irish Jurist,* Vol. 5 Parts I and II 1970 to be continued in Vol. 6 Part I 1971, *The Founding of Dáil Éireann,* Dublin 1971.

[4]N. Mansergh, *The Irish Free State: its government and politics,* London 1934, 174.

[5]Interview 'Lemass on Government' in *Léargas,* no. 12, January-February 1968, 3.

[6]M. Ó Muimhneacháin, *The Functions of the Department of the Taoiseach,* Dublin 1960, 19. Cf. *Report of the Public Services Organisation Review Group, 1966-1969* ('The Devlin Report'), chap. 19, 206-210.

[7]Donal O'Sullivan, *The Irish Free State and its Senate,* London 1940, 6. For similar views see J. L. McCracken, *Representative Government in Ireland,* Oxford 1958, 90; Basil Chubb, *Government and Politics of Ireland,* Oxford 1970, 168.

2

W. T. Cosgrave

Cosgrave became leader by accident. The deaths of Griffith
and Collins in rapid succession, just as the new state was
being created, left a vacancy that had to be filled quickly
and uncontroversially. Cosgrave was not the immediately
obvious choice. The first name put forward to take over
the reins of government was that of Richard Mulcahy. This
original nomination by Kevin O'Higgins made sense in those
troubled days of Civil War. Mulcahy's status would have
guaranteed the continued loyal allegiance of the Army and
could have postponed the still unresolved question of the
constitutional control of that Army. Moreover Mulcahy's
appointment might have persuaded some uncertain dissidents
on the other side that the new Provisional Government was
committed to Collins's 'stepping stone' policy and to the full
realisation of Sinn Féin national ideals. On the other hand
it was argued and accepted that the accession of any military
leader in succession to Collins would militate against the
creation of a 'normal' political situation in the new state.

Once Mulcahy had been passed over, Cosgrave was the
inevitable choice. Among party leaders only MacNeill could
have been regarded as more senior and he was never fully
acceptable as a leader after 1916. Cosgrave had a national
record stretching back before 1916 and a long experience in
politics. One of the earliest victors in the Sinn Féin by-
elections and a member of the Dáil from the outset, Cosgrave
became Minister for Local Government in April 1919,
immediately after his release from gaol, and continued
throughout the period to serve in the cabinet. During the

absence of Collins, earlier in 1922, Cosgrave chaired the meetings of the Provisional Government. It might be noted in passing that in Britain in 1923 Lord Curzon regarded an invitation to preside at the cabinet in the Prime Minister's absence as 'more than a mere formality; it was an indication, it was a promise'. The promise was not fulfilled: Stanley Baldwin succeeded Bonar Law.[1]

At first Cosgrave had little opportunity to exhibit strong executive power within the cabinet. He did not aspire to be a charismatic leader. He had inherited a team and continued to speak in terms of cabinet rather than personal leadership. Cosgrave publicly associated his governmental colleagues with decisions, including even the choice of ministers. He told the Dáil in 1923 that in filling the portfolio of Finance he consulted the members of the Executive Council and, with their approval, offered the post to Blythe. Later in the same debate he returned to the same point:

> Last year when making up the Ministry I consulted with the other ministers. It was within the period known as the Provisional Parliament in the Third Dáil, and I got their advice and assistance, and I took the advice and counsel separately of some of the ministers—I think more than of any other that of the Minister for Agriculture.
>
> (*Dáil Debates* 5/48, 20 September 1923.)

This insistence on invoking Hogan, who was technically an 'extern' minister, seems to underline Cosgrave's perception of his role as that of chairman. Later in 1923 he gave a further insight into his attitude towards the selection of ministers:

> I may say for my own part that, in considering this question of offering portfolios to ministers, or in asking members to take up the responsibilities of office, I had in mind always the man's own desires or capabilities for these particular posts.
>
> (*Dáil Debates* 5/1409, 5 December 1923.)

Much later, in the debate on the 1937 Constitution,

C   19

Cosgrave spelled out his opinion on the appropriate relationship between head of government and cabinet colleagues:

> We have had experience for fifteen years of the independence of ministers of state. In this new Constitution that no longer obtains. The Prime Minister has been given pre-eminent position and power. In theory, a case may be made for the exaltation of the Prime Minister as distinct from other ministers of state. In practice, and I have had a longer experience of its practice than anybody else in the country, it was not open to the Prime Minister to ask for and compel the resignation of a minister, nor was it open to him to demand and so secure the resignation of the Attorney-General. Ministers, in my view, ought to possess security and a measure of independence. In my view, the Attorney-General also occupies a position, and should occupy in this state a position, in which he should not be subject to political dominion or direction. He should fulfil the duties of his office, and the administration with which he is charged, with almost judicial discretion and independence.
>
> (*Dáil Debates* 68/348, 14 June 1937.)

This remarkably reductive doctrine of prime ministerial power was echoed in the remarks of former ministers during the same debate. McGilligan argued that the dismissal of ministers should be a function of the government as a whole, rather than a prerogative of its leader. A former Attorney-General and subsequent Taoiseach, J. A. Costello, submitted that:

> Under the existing Constitution the President of the Executive Council is merely a member of the Executive Council. The Executive Council is the government of this state with collective responsibility and each and every minister has a dignity and responsibility.
>
> (*Dáil Debates* 67/301, 12 May 1937.)

Of course none of these statements should be construed too rigorously; the broad sweep of theory must be modified by

20

the recognition that Cosgrave and his Fine Gael colleagues in this debate were concerned to contrast their sense of government as a collectivity with the presumed one-man dominance of de Valera. Cosgrave's performance in office reveals a more robust leadership. While he inherited his governmental team it is worth noting that in his first Executive Council he demoted Eamon Duggan, one of the signatories of the Treaty who had been Minister for Home Affairs under Griffith, to the rank of parliamentary secretary. Five years later by a similar decisive action Cosgrave moved James Burke from his position as Minister for Local Government and Public Health and named him Parliamentary Secretary to Finance.

Cosgrave's period in office was one of the most turbulent and tortuous that any political leader could experience. Neither a demagogue nor an extremist, he had to play mid-wife to the difficult birth-pangs of the new state, pushing through a wide range of legislation—much of it aridly institutional but vitally necessary to the establishment of an independent Irish administration—while an expectant people discovered that the fruits of independence were less immediately sweet and certainly less profitable than many had supposed. Courts, police, bureaucracy were covered in Acts which have remained basic to the framework of the Irish state. Yet in these earliest foundation years of the state there were no established and clear-cut party lines to give stability.

Two large groupings of opinion, each an amalgamation of differing interests and aspirations cut off from the earlier Sinn Féin movement, confronted each other in a short but bitter and expensive Civil War. Neither side was a party in any conventional sense; political leaders in each had difficulty controlling and containing the militants on their own side. Indeed the very idea of organised and disciplined political parties suffered, in the eyes of many Irish voters, both from association with the recently discredited Irish Parliamentary Party and from a barrage of criticism aimed at the artificiality of the British two-party system. The constitutional founders of the Irish Free State had neither anticipated nor desired such organised parties. They expected to have small groups in the

Dáil representing various interests and grouping together to represent their own constituents and to control executive action. But from the outset it was evident that some mechanism was required to aggregate opinion in the new state and help achieve political stability. That need was even greater given an extended period during which the very legitimacy of the new régime was denied by a large, determined, organised minority. The actual organisation of the Irish party system is discussed in Maurice Manning's *Irish Political Parties* in the present series. The point to be made here, simply, is that Cosgrave's capacity to survive as leader during this troubled decade is itself a measure of his political acumen and strength within his cabinet.

In these ten years a major legislative programme was required to shape and fashion the new Ireland. An early observer of this process of reconstruction has commented :

> Acts were passed dealing with the organisation of local government, the land problem, pensions, beef-sugar subsidies, police, the civil service, the courts, currency, electricity supply, fisheries, housing, intoxicating liquors, railways, roads, tariffs and unemployment. In the field of external affairs the Irish government successfully pressed its claim for a greater degree of independence than was formally described in the constitutional law of the British Empire. After the revolution there was an effort to build up popular support for the constitution and, though this achievement was in itself notable enough, the government propagandists have exaggerated the claims. The principal criticism in the face of these claims is that the Cosgrave government neglected social services and failed to do its part in improving the economic condition of the country.[2]

However it might be suggested that this kind of criticism needs to be placed both against Cosgrave's own consciously conservative attitudes and against the dangers that haunted every step of the first five years in particular.

The effort, for instance, to establish firmly civilian control over a considerably reduced national Army provoked a serious cabinet and political crisis in March 1924. Civil control of the armed forces has long been recognised as one of the most difficult problems for new states born out of national liberation struggles and to place the Irish experience against that of other countries is illuminating in many ways for an understanding of Irish political culture and development. Although the Irish 'Army Crisis' stretched back over many months, the first public intimation of trouble came with the resignation of Joseph McGrath from the cabinet and the publication of an ultimatum from a group of senior Army officers demanding 'a conference with representatives of your government to discuss our interpretation of the Treaty'. An already delicate and dangerous situation was further aggravated when G.H.Q. officers, acting under orders of the Minister of Defence, Richard Mulcahy, conducted a raid to round up 'mutineers' without either the knowledge or approval of the civilian government or of its newly appointed head of the armed forces, General Eoin O'Duffy. The continued influence of competing I.R.B. and I.R.A. elements in the Army undoubtedly lay behind these events. Yet despite the military and political risks involved, the Cosgrave administration did not hesitate. All officers involved, no matter how senior or close to cabinet members, were removed. The Minister for Defence's own position was now dangerously exposed. McGrath openly blamed him for trouble in the Army: in the cabinet, other colleagues, notably O'Higgins, were equally critical. After nearly two exhausting years in office as leader, (much of it actually spent living in Government Buildings) Cosgrave's own health had collapsed. Kevin O'Higgins told the Dáil later:

> I had in my hand a letter from the President's physician stating that he was not to be worried about public matters, and that interviews, correspondence, or even telephone messages were to be avoided as far as possible.
>
> (*Dáil Debates* 7/3155, 26 June 1924.)

Nevertheless, the cabinet sent urgently to suggest that Mulcahy's resignation be demanded; while Cosgrave was agreeing a letter of resignation arrived from the Minister for Defence. Even then the political crisis was not over. McGrath continued to agitate and in October 1924 led eight other government back-benchers to resign from the Dáil. It says much for the public approval accorded to Cosgrave's leadership that Cumann na nGael won seven of the nine resulting by-elections on 13 March 1925. The whole episode was indicative of the extraordinary degree of stability achieved by the new régime, of the legitimacy attached to its civilian leaders, and of the undisputed leadership role of Cosgrave.

Similarly, in November 1925, when the premature and unauthorised publication of the Boundary Commission's findings made Eoin MacNeill's position untenable, the Cosgrave cabinet was able to survive the resignation of yet another senior minister and the political odium associated with an unpopular enforced partition. It is still not clear whether MacNeill's resignation was demanded (and, if so, whether O'Higgins might not—as in the Mulcahy case—have been more demanding than Cosgrave) or tendered by MacNeill himself. However the case is mentioned here less as evidence of Cosgrave's control over individual members of the cabinet and more as an indicator of the ease with which the leader had made himself politically indispensable.

This unassailable position of leadership was further underlined following the assassination of O'Higgins two years later. For if the simple judgment of the Army crisis is accepted that 'O'Higgins, Vice-President of the Executive Council, handled the affair and emerged as the strong man of the cabinet'[3] one needs to explain how Cosgrave managed to survive politically after O'Higgins' death. The plain truth seems to be that O'Higgins' strength has been exaggerated and Cosgrave's under-estimated. For despite an unstable electoral situation—two general elections within three months in 1927—despite the rise of the powerful new Fianna Fáil party, despite even a governmental defeat in the Dáil in March 1930 and a slender government majority throughout, Cosgrave was never dislodged from his role as leader, nor even seriously challenged. In September 1927 his prestige allowed him to stand for both Cork Borough and the Carlow-Kilkenny constituency; he was returned for both areas. It should also be noticed that a complicating factor in this election was J. J. Walsh's sudden and embarrassing withdrawal from politics shortly after his appointment to the Executive Council in June 1927.

Cosgrave selected the first generation of post-independence senior civil servants, as well as over-seeing the establishment of the formal institutions of the state. He carried through Griffith's policy of reconciling Southern Unionists to the new régime by his nominations to the first Senate. He asserted the head of government's control over parliamentary time. Consciously playing the role of chairman rather than chief, Cosgrave nevertheless survived more frequent and serious cabinet crises than any of his successors in office. He held together a group whose views on policy were by no means unanimous; Werner Moss commented in 1933 :

> Cumann na nGael's tariff policy has never been clearly defined and the Cosgrave cabinet contained men who ranged all the way from the extreme protectionist views of Mr. Walsh, Minister for Posts and Telegraphs, to the free-trade views of Mr. Hogan, the Minister for Agriculture.[4]

Early members of Cumann na nGael are adamant that Cosgrave was in reality, as well as in informal title, 'the Boss'. It would require a full-scale study to assess the performance of Cosgrave as head of government but even this short summary indicates the inadequacy of the conventionally accepted account of the first President of the Executive Council.

NOTES: W. T. Cosgrave

[1]H. Nicolson, *Curzon: the Last Phase,* London 1934, 353.
[2]W. Moss, *Political Parties in the Irish Free State,* New York 1933, p. 24, note 8.
[3]Carlton Younger, *Ireland's Civil War,* Fontana Books, 512.
[4]Moss. *op. cit.,* 29.

25

3

Eamon de Valera

De Valera has been such a powerful political figure for so long that it is difficult to recover the origins of his influence and standing. He emerged initially, in the aftermath of the Easter Rising, as President of the newly re-organised Sinn Féin party in 1917. De Valera was a compromise choice between the more conservatively constitutional group of original Sinn Féin men led by Arthur Griffith and a newer and more militant grouping nominally led by Count Plunkett. The new Sinn Féin was, indeed, even less cohesive than this description implies; it is examined in *The Founding of Dáil Éireann* in this series of studies.

Undoubtedly, de Valera developed a considerable political expertise and personal *charisma,* but in those early days many still considered him a political innocent. In May 1918, William O'Brien, M.P., wrote to Tim Healy that John Dillon had invited de Valera to his home in Ballaghadereen and commented: 'de Valera is personally a charming as well as an honest man but he is too good for this rough world of old Parliamentary hands and will no doubt subside into a meek instrument of Dillon's.'[1] The judgement was wide off the mark but is quoted here as an indication of the extent to which, as yet, de Valera was an unknown and unreckoned political force.

In the course of the Treaty debate—to summarise and simplify a complex situation—he seems to have been pushed into a more rigid and doctrinaire stand than he would have wished by some of his followers. Subsequently, in founding Fianna Fáil and wooing a majority of recalcitrant 'repub-

26

licans' back into parliamentary policies, de Valera helped to confirm the stable, constitutional direction of the independent Irish state.

It was an immense task and was not achieved without a great organisational effort. It was not a one-man job but the work of an experienced team of political managers and leaders. The senior members included: Seán T. O'Kelly (already an established Sinn Féin leader when he was elected to the first Dáil); Seán MacEntee and James Ryan (whose national record also stretched back beyond the Sinn Féin election of December 1918 to the Easter Rising); Frank Aiken and Oscar Traynor (regional commandants of the I.R.A. during the War of Independence) and—most energetic and effective of all—Seán Lemass and Gerry Boland (who became first Honorary Secretaries of the Fianna Fáil party). When he formed his first cabinet in 1932 de Valera was surrounded by these comrades and political organisation men. They remained together in government, bound by ties of loyalty and inter-dependence, until the late fifties. Replacements into the middle forties tended to be chosen from the same stable of early followers and their families; there was no effort to recruit the governmental elite from any wider field.

Undoubtedly de Valera dominated his team. It is going too far to say he dictated. He explained himself:

It was said that these were 'yes-men'. It is very easy to make a general statement of this sort whenever a team is working harmoniously together. When we have discussed and differed and come to a conclusion in advance, as we do, it is very easy to suggest, because they are loyal—having accepted a decision—that in putting it into effect they are only 'yes-men'. Some of these men were in the National Movement before I was. They are men of independent mind and character.

(*Dáil Debates* 91/217; 2 July 1943.)

Nevertheless when it came to allocating offices, de Valera exercised his own judgement. Lemass has reported of the 1932 choice that there was no prior consultation, no questioning of ministers expressing preference for particular posts; he himself was only told his office half an hour before it was announced to the Dáil. Lemass has commented that:

De Valera always struck me as having much more concern in picking people for ministerial posts with his own personal regard for them rather than his assessment of their capacity to do that particular job . . . he made up his own mind and certainly, to my mind, he was not the best of judges of the capacity of individuals to do particular categories of work.

De Valera's own political interests were limited, in the main, to an important but narrow band of constitutional questions concerning relations with Britain. Within that group of cabinet ministers and associates these were not controversial issues. Beyond this, more particularly in economic and in large measure in social areas, de Valera was content to leave policy to the others, while he maintained his own vision of frugal rural self-sufficiency. He spelled out his ideal in a radio broadcast on St. Patrick's Day, 1943:

The Ireland which we have dreamed of would be the home of a people who valued material wealth only as a basis of a right living, of a people who were satisfied with frugal comfort and devoted their leisure to the things of the spirit; a land whose countryside would be bright with cosy homesteads, whose fields and villages would be joyous with the sounds of industry, with the romping of sturdy children, the contests of athletic youths, the laughter of comely maidens; whose firesides would be forums for the wisdom of old age. It would, in a word, be the home of a people living the life that God desires men should live.

While de Valera nurtured his ideals it was the urban members of the cabinet—Lemass, O'Kelly, MacEntee—who shaped much of the real direction of government priorities and the allocation of resources. De Valera himself regretted the growth of government intervention and said so frequently in the Dáil. Even after World War II he could say:

28

The Government, and legislation generally, have nowadays to intervene very much in what would be regarded as the private concerns of the individual.

(*Dáil Debates* 99/1891; 1 March 1946.)

He seemed to favour exhortation as a mode of public leadership, even for complex problems; in a revealing comment during the debate on the adjournment in 1933 he said:

The Cabinet as a whole has time after time come back to this question of unemployment, and I for one, at any rate, have come to the conclusion that, if we are to make an effort to deal with unemployment we will have to deal with it in the spirit of crusaders.

(*Dáil Debates* 46/2654; 7 April 1933.)

This attitude perhaps explains what might otherwise be regarded as executive indolence in some policy areas. Despite his own passionate attachment to the revival of Irish, little was done to divert large-scale governmental resources under de Valera. He explained:

the restoration of the language depends more upon the attitude of the people outside than upon the attitude of the public representatives here. Public representatives can do a tremendous lot in giving a lead, in helping the people, in explaining to them the importance of this matter as a national objective. Unfortunately, again, it is not one of those things which a government can do by a wave of the wand.

(*Dáil Debates* 112/2430; 6 August 1948.)

Hence an inert policy in education was tolerated without any change of minister. De Valera preferred, it was said, to run the department himself in addition to his other responsibilities. It was left to the first inter-party government to establish a separate Department of the Gaeltacht.

By all accounts of senior colleagues an excessively patient chairman, de Valera was also inclined—certainly in later years—to bring unannounced detail to cabinets and insist that

29

these take precedence over items on the agenda. As a mode of leadership his chairmanship must on occasions have been infuriating. It was certainly a far cry from the common Opposition criticism of one-man rule. De Valera managed cabinet and party disagreements by a process of attrition. He pursued agreement, and preferably unanimity, without regard to either the significance of the particular decision or to considerations of time; remorselessly insistent, agonisingly tolerant of the irrelevant and the long-winded, meticulous in the drafting of formulae, his strategy was to allow opposition to burn itself out rather than confront it with superior support. Lemass later described de Valera's method to Michael Mills in the *Irish Press*:

> He had a different technique to mine. He relied upon the force of physical exhaustion to get agreement. In other words he'd never let a cabinet debate on any subject end with a vote of ministers.
>
> He always wanted to get unanimity and he sought this unanimity by the simple process of keeping the debate going—often till the small hours of the morning, until those who were in the minority, out of sheer exhaustion, conceded the case made by the majority. This technique was quite effective in his case.

Indeed, it may be that it was the leadership style as much as the personality of the man which gave the later de Valera governments such a conservative colouring; they moved slowly, at the pace of the last man to be convinced.

In the 1937 Constitution debate de Valera was explicit about his views on government leadership. If there was sharp disagreement in the cabinet it was best to postpone decision; if the issue was urgent then perhaps the Taoiseach should see unconvinced ministers individually; he himself preferred 'substantial unanimity'. He queried whether it was the practice of Fine Gael when in office 'to have questions decided by a majority of the Executive Council? If so I think it was a bad practice'. (*Dáil Debates* 67/1175; 26 May 1937.) He also registered the significant fact that he had made enquiries

30

and could only discover one case in the previous government in which a member of the Executive Council asked to be put down as dissenting : although Deputy Fitzgerald-Kenny, a former Minister for Justice, countered that very few cabinet decisions required a vote because all ministers were members of the same party.

The debate on the Fifth Stage, as James Dillon noted, followed 'an unusual procedure' and de Valera addressed himself at some length to the question of role of the envisaged Taoiseach as against that of the existent President of the Executive Council :

The fact is that he is not being put in any stronger position than the position the President of the Executive Council had occupied here in practice during these periods.

Deputy Cosgrave said that the Prime Minister ought not to be in such a position as to be able to force the resignation of a colleague. Of course he was always in that position. Because if one of the ministers was acting in such a way that it was not possible to carry on with the team, the President would have to speak to him and say : 'There is a difficulty here; how are we going to manage it? Either you see eye to eye with us or you are definitely opposed to us; we are not a Coalition Government; we cannot carry on as a team'. If that minister did not resign, then naturally the President would see the other members of the Government and talk to them on the matter. Finally, if this particular minister were so conducting himself that the carrying on of the Government would not have been possible, the President would easily have got him out of Government. He would, of course, have to use a cumbersome process. He would have to come down to the Dáil and resign, and his whole government would have to resign. If he had sufficient strength with his government he would have to re-form that government without the particular minister that he objected to.

Now, is it right that there should be such a round-about process for something which could be done in a straight-

31

forward manner? The suggestion is that these things could be done in the dark. They could not be done in the dark. No head of a government can get rid of one of his colleagues without the fact being known. Someone must be appointed in his place. If they go before the Parliament as a body the matter will have to be raised, and if that member was strong enough in the old position to prevent the President of the Executive Council from forcing him to resign, he would be strong enough in the new position. Both are really the same thing. It is a question of whether the particular minister has a majority of the Executive Council or a majority of the Dáil or not. For that reason I say that what has been done in the past is now being translated into practice. The President of the Executive Council in the past was elected by the Dáil. He was made responsible for the election of his team. He selected that team, he was responsible for keeping that team together, and he was expected to keep uniformity so far as that could be done. He was the central pivot on which the whole Government was arranged. The duty placed on him by the Dáil was to see that the team was kept together as a unit and that it worked as a unit. It was his responsibility to see if he was unable to perform that duty that the Dáil was made aware of it so as to make it right again. That is the position that is here.

It is suggested that the Taoiseach will have power in future to get a dissolution without going to his colleagues first. It is nonsense to think that any Taoiseach will do that. The whole Party, including the Taoiseach, will have to go up for election. He will have to be supported by the majority of his colleagues, and normally he cannot and will not force a dissolution against their will. If he were to do that, the Taoiseach would be breaking up his party and prejudicing the chances of either himself or his colleagues getting back again as Government. The difference between the new and the old constitutional position is this: that everybody can clearly see the new constitutional position, and it is not hidden away.

32

It puts upon the individual the direct responsibility of keeping his team as a team, and where necessary bringing pressure on that particular member to leave the Government. He can only do this in practice if supported by the majority of the party. Clearly he could not do it without the support of the majority of his party.

There is therefore in the Constitution nothing to justify the suggestion that the office of President is one of dictatorship and that the Prime Minister is put in a position over and above that which he occupies at present. This is only making explicit what was implicit all the time so far as the Taoiseach is concerned.

(*Dáil Debates* 68/420-423; 14 June 1937.)

Earlier in the same debate, speaking in Irish, de Valera cut through the conventional rhetoric on the power of parliament to emphasise the reality of executive power in blunt terms:

The government will have the greatest power in the State. The government will be answerable to the Dáil from day to day. But if it were not for the majority of the Dáil the Government would not be ruling at all, and since the Dáil is elected by the people, and the government by the representatives of the people, it is right in my opinion that this group should have this power. If anyone wants to discover where the power of the State is located, he will find it is in the government. The government has power—as much power as it has had up to now. The government cannot conduct its business without this power.

(*Dáil Debates* 67/35; 11 May 1937. My translation.)

Clearly, de Valera understood and accepted what A. H. Birch has so well identified as 'the Whitehall model' of parliamentary government. The same perception of the concentration of executive power and responsibility in the Irish system made de Valera a firm apostle of strong party discipline. He rejected the idea of free votes in parliament. Speaking on the vote on the Taoiseach's Department in 1951, he said: 'I think that free votes where a Government is concerned are

33

wrong. . . . I am not a lover of the idea of free votes. I believe that the government are responsible for deciding and making up their minds on questions of national policy'. (*Dáil Debates* 126/2028; 19 July 1951.)

The previous year, speaking on the Criminal Justice Bill, he had elaborated his views:

> I believe that the government and the minister are not doing their duty by the House in allowing matters of this magnitude to be decided by a free vote. . . . The government is bound to consider in advance serious matters of this sort and to arrive at a decision upon them. Having come to a decision, they should try to press that decision, if they believe it right, with all their might upon the members of the House.
>
> (*Dáil Debates* 123/589; 9 November 1950.)

In the same way, whether in or out of office, he was a jealous upholder of the convention of executive secrecy and collective responsibility. Yet de Valera was also capable of an almost American emphasis on the separation of powers: speaking on the Committee Stage of the Criminal Justice Bill in 1950 he asserted:

> I find myself on practically all occasions opposed to the idea of conferring on the Executive, particularly on an individual member of the Executive, powers to override decisions of the courts. There are safeguards to justice in having independent courts. We have many times prided ourselves on the fact that our courts are independent of the Executive, on having independent courts and having hearings in public. Both of these principles are affected when we give to a member of the Executive power to override the decisions of the courts. He is a member of the Executive. Therefore the separation of powers upon which we pride ourselves so much is affected by it.
>
> (*Dáil Debates* 123/586; 9 November 1950.)

However, this was said when in Opposition and, more often

than not, de Valera was in government. His performance there offers more useful clues to his real attitudes to executive power. There were, of course, cabinet disagreement. They were not permitted to ruffle the placid waters of internal Irish politics during de Valera's period of office; the infection of disagreement was never allowed to gather into a crisis point. He met differences of opinion either by exhaustive group discussions or by direct confrontation with the individual minister involved. He was known to send for papers and for civil servants from departments but, more commonly, was willing to leave senior ministers alone to run their own departments. In 1947, with an almost text-book nicety, he explained to the Dáil the theory of collective responsibility and of individual ministerial responsibility.

Deputies must realise that we are organised as Departments and that each Department does its own planning. That planning is then synthesised or integrated at Government meetings, where the Departments are, so to speak, represented . . . in our constitutional theory here, every minister is directly responsible to the House for his own Department. He has an individual responsibility, and he cannot cover himself in his responsibility by saying that something is Government policy. . . . I am mainly responsible for the integration of the work of all Departments.

(*Dáil Debates* 107/756; 2 July 1947.)

In practice de Valera usually stood over his ministers, or at least, did not use his immense prestige to apply this theory of individual ministerial responsibility in its full rigour.

Even the various cabinet shuffles of the period give little indication of whether the Taoiseach was expressing approval or disapproval of his ministers' performance. Indeed some senior ministers report themselves still puzzled by some of the departmental moves; some of the suggested explanations of cabinet shuffles fail to convince. Nor is there very strong evidence that de Valera made use of the two strongest weapons in the Taoiseach's armoury : the right to dismiss ministers and the right to determine the timing of elections. On the latter, he consulted colleagues—inevitably, perhaps, since they were (as already indicated above) the real managers of the party.

However, there appears to be some conflict of evidence on this point with regard to the January 1933 election. De Valera's most recent biographers state that the decision

> was taken by de Valera alone. He sent for each minister individually and informed him of his decision. It came to them as a great surprise, as they had not suffered a defeat in the House and a dissolution might in fact jeopardise the position of the party.[2]

One experienced lobby correspondent has gone even further to assert that

> when de Valera declared a general election in January 1933, the entire cabinet rebelled, believing that they would be heavily defeated, Dev said not to worry : they would get a bigger majority than ever.[3]

Two senior cabinet officers of the period have denied this version in conversations with the present author. They make the point that the election was in fact already anticipated, and inevitable, once the *détente* between the government and the Labour Party leaders broke down. During 1932 an arrangement had been made to hold weekly meetings between Norton and other Labour deputies and members of the government. The intention was to make Labour familiar with governmental intentions and, presumably, permit them to influence proposed legislation. The scheme was not successful since Labour used information gained at these meetings to 'demand' legislation which was already in the pipeline and thus exaggerate its influence on policy and win political credit. The break came with a proposal to cut Civil Service salaries (then related to the cost of living) as the economic slump depressed prices. Following publication of an article on the topic in the Post Office Workers' Union bulletin the weekly meetings were discontinued. Lemass indeed has spoken of a sense of relief when the Fianna Fáil-Labour understanding began to break down; de Valera told him of Norton's

36

warning that Labour would vote against the wages cut and asked his advice. Lemass did not hesitate: 'I'd dissolve the Dáil before they got a chance of voting and have another election.' De Valera agreed and the election was held.

As for dismissals, there are only six possible cases, and since we have so little definite evidence it seems best to deal with them in simple chronological sequence.

Following the 1933 General Election, de Valera did not reinstate his first Minister for Justice, James Geoghegan. It is difficult to see this as an example of ministerial sacking. It is true that Geoghegan was one of the two members of the first de Valera administration who had not been a founder-member of Fianna Fáil; he was, indeed, a relative newcomer to the political arena first standing at the Longford-West-meath by-election in 1930 at the age of forty-four. This might suggest that he would be an easy minister to drop; on the other hand, his subsequent appointment as Attorney-General for less than two months in 1936 and thence to the Supreme Court seems to fit the more general view that politics was an intermission in a professional legal career and that Geoghegan himself wanted to relinquish his governmental portfolio, return to the Bar and begin his ascent to the Bench.

The second case was in May 1936. With the abolition of the Senate, the Minister for Lands and Fisheries, Senator Joseph Connolly, was forced to leave the government. Although he had been leader of the Senate and had served as one of the five ex-Senators on the 'Second House of the Oireachtas' Committee, in the subsequent reconstitution of Seanad Éireann he was not brought back either into the Senate or the government. It is known that Senator Connolly was an argumentative cabinet colleague and unhappy about the direction of domestic policy; both 'conservative' and 'progressive' ministers of the period agreed on the point. Connolly himself certainly came to believe that he had been virtually 'sacked', although it is by no means certain that he could have won a Dáil seat in his own right. And, as far as the general public was concerned, there was no question of an open break, still less of punishment, in the handling of the case. Connolly

37

was appointed Chairman of the Commissioners of Public Works.

In August 1941 the resignation of P. J. Ruttledge, Minister for Local Government and Public Health, was accepted. There seems no reason to doubt that genuine grounds of ill-health then given. Ruttledge had already been removed from the Department of Justice (to which he had been appointed in succession to Geoghegan in 1933) in the reorganisation of the cabinet at the outbreak of the war. Information from his successor published in the *Irish Times* series 'Gerry Boland's Story' suggests that 'a tough man was needed because of the serious illness of Mr. Ruttledge. . . . Mr. de Valera called in Mr. Boland, gave him an idea of the stern policy needed and then asked him to take on that tough, "dirty" job. Boland could not refuse Dev—they had been colleagues for too long.' (*Irish Times*, 14 October 1968.)

In 1946 Dr. Conor Ward resigned his post of Parliamentary Secretary to the Minister for Local Government and Public Health which he had held for fourteen years, because of allegations made against him regarding a business transaction in a bacon factory. Especially in view of Dr. Ward's central responsibility for the government's proposed, and controversial, new health policy, it is clear that to continue in office would have been politically damaging to the government. But there are sufficient clues to show that Dr. Ward intended to ride out the storm, if possible. The available evidence indicates that the resignation was demanded by de Valera.

After the first period of inter-party government, P. J. Little was not reinstated in the Department of Posts and Telegraphs to which he had been appointed in 1939. By 1951, of course, Little was in his later sixties. However, age alone was scarcely the determining factor : Boland was only a year younger and de Valera himself was two years older than Little. Former colleagues have agreed that in this case a minister was pushed (although very gently) from office.

Similarly after the second period of inter-party government, Gerry Boland was not made a member of government.

In this case we know a little more about the circumstances. The Political Correspondent of the *Irish Times*, Michael McInerney, has recorded that :

> (Boland) then spoke sadly of Dev's great victory in 1957, and of his own departure from the cabinet. One day Dev called him in and told him that he was thinking of putting his son, Kevin, in the Government. Kevin who had not been a member of the Oireachtas had been on the Executive (of the Fianna Fáil party) for a few years, and Dev had a high opinion of him. 'That was the first I had heard of this, and my reply to him was : "So you want to get rid of me. I've been talking my mind too much for you, I suppose." But although I was hurt at ending my 25 years in leadership, I was pleased really, and anyway I was getting on a bit then, so I told Dev to ring up Kevin himself; he did so.' (*Irish Times,* 19 October 1968.)

Circumstantial evidence bears out this version of de Valera using his political patronage, as in Connolly's case. Kevin Boland was appointed to the Department of Defence in 1957. This was the only occasion—with the exception of Dr. Noel Browne's appointment to the Department of Health in 1948 —when a deputy, on his first day in the Dáil, had been appointed to the Cabinet. Moreover, the Boland appointment involved passing over three Parliamentary Secretaries (D. Ó Briain, P. Beegan, M. J. Kennedy) who had been appointed in 1951. Perhaps too much should not be made of this point. In the 1957 Cabinet, Blaney, Moran and Ormonde were all given ministries without previous experience as parliamentary secretaries; they were all, of course, deputies of long standing (Blaney first elected 1948; Moran 1936; Ormonde 1947).

Taking all these cases, it is evident that de Valera had none of that taste for ministerial butchery which R. A. Butler suggested is an essential part of the equipment of a modern British Prime Minister. In no more than four of the cases is it possible to speak of a resignation, or non-reinstatement, as forced. Clearly de Valera was reluctant and perhaps excessively gentle in using his powers of dismissal. Where action was required the pill was sweetened—an alternative post and status provided. Nothing was done in a hurry. It might be argued that by this technique de Valera exhibited his consummate political ability, maintaining old loyalties (and their supports) and permanently preserving the facade of party unity. On the other hand, it must be acknowledged that the approach had the institutional effect of curtailing the development of the Taoiseach's control over his cabinet. De Valera's unwillingness to use openly his constitutional right to 'hire and fire' has made it more difficult for his successors to discipline cabinet colleagues, has contributed to a certain caution in replacing ministers and, arguably, has made the task of enforcing true collective responsibility under a single head a more constant concern than it might otherwise be.

Finally, in considering de Valera's performance as head of government there is even some doubt about how it came to an end. The question has been asked in the British context whether senior cabinet colleagues could force the retirement of a Prime Minister. In de Valera's case it has been suggested that the decision to relinquish his executive office in favour of the Presidency in 1959 may have been urged upon him by colleagues. According to an account in *NUSIGHT* news magazine, during 1968

Even some of his closest colleagues had begun to feel that he was no longer physically fit to be Taoiseach, especially with the new demands of government direction of economic development. . . . Consequently, in late '58 Ryan and MacEntee convened a top-secret meeting of Cabinet Ministers where the issue of Dev's retirement was discussed. All agreed with the exception of Frank Aiken that Dev should be approached and asked to stand for the Presidency in June of the following year. Again, MacEntee and Ryan went to Dev, told him of the consensus within the cabinet and Dev agreed to go. (December 1959.)

A more recent account occurs in the Appreciation of Dr. J. Ryan in the *Irish Times* and identifies Ryan as the man who went to Dev in early 1957 and suggested he ought to stand as a candidate for the Presidency. Dev knew what he meant and just said: 'If the Party wants that, then I am ready to go.' But two hearts were near broken at the short conversation, for it meant that Dev was to leave politics—his life. (26 September 1970.)

Seán MacEntee has totally denied the first report and the second scarcely adds up to pressure by senior colleagues. Indeed, it is difficult to see quite where this pressure would originate.

De Valera himself had been openly talking of retiring for some time and had clearly identified Lemass as his successor. Many senior ministers must have recognised that when this change occurred the end of their own term would be in sight. At the same time, it was clear that de Valera's eyesight now left him more than ever dependent upon other people's reports and there was a general acceptance of the transition to the presidency as a suitable ending to a distinguished career in Irish politics. It may well be that de Valera himself was conscious that Lemass, like Eden in the British context, had been playing the role of second-in-command too long. On balance, then, it appears that de Valera relinquished office of his own accord; it seems unlikely that any significant section of the cabinet either wished or had the power to force that decision on him.

Both Cosgrave and de Valera were in charge of single-party governments. Even when dependent for parliamentary majorities on the support of other parties, they tended to act with the full authority of majority leaders. The third incumbent, John A. Costello, faced a radically different parliamentary situation which conditioned and circumscribed his role as Taoiseach.

NOTES: Eamon de Valera

[1]William O'Brien papers. National Library of Ireland, Ms 8556/19 2 May 1918.

[2]Earl of Longford, T. P. O'Neill *Eamon de Valera*, Gill & Macmillan 1970, p. 287.

[3]Appreciation of Dr. J. Ryan in *Irish Times*, 26 September 1970.

4

J. A. Costello

The first inter-party government of 1948 was not merely a widely based grouping. It contained the whole range of parliamentary representation with the solitary exception of Fianna Fáil. Its *raison d'être* indeed was simply the exclusion of the largest party from executive office after an unbroken tenure of sixteen years. The span of five parties included in the government comprised: a Fine Gael party still largely identified as conservative and middle class, together with its break-away former vice-president and future leader, James Dillon; the two parliamentary divisions of the Labour Party (Labour and National Labour); the new radical republican-socialist coalition of Clann na Poblachta, headed by former I.R.A. chief of staff Seán MacBride; the Western-oriented Clann na Talmhan. Even this grouping required the support of Independent deputies to form a majority.

The man chosen as head of this precariously united government of disparates had never held ministerial office. The selection of Costello, a former Attorney-General and distinguished senior counsel, in place of the Fine Gael party leader, General Richard Mulcahy, has given a flavour of authenticity to the story that the new government grew out of a 'Bar Library plot.' Additional backing is given by the fact that two senior ministries were also held by lawyers (Finance: Patrick McGilligan; External Affairs: Seán MacBride) and the government chief whip, Liam Cosgrave, was also a member of the Bar. In fact the prime mover in creating this new governmental experiment in Ireland was Mulcahy.

The general election was held on Wednesday, 4 February

1948. A record total of 406 candidates and the death of a candidate on polling day slowed down the counting of votes and declaration of results. The national results were not clear until Tuesday, 10 February. On the following day, a week after polling day, Mulcahy wrote to the leaders of the other four parties inviting them to a meeting in Leinster House on the afternoon of Friday 13. All attended except National Labour. Mulcahy's suggestions for a broad allocation of ministries between parties were accepted but Norton intimated that Labour would not accept the leader of any other party as head of government. This was almost certainly a tactful way of registering objection to Mulcahy's obvious claim to become Taoiseach. Mulcahy, while pointing out that Fine Gael supporters would legitimately expect their leader to head the government, gave an immediate assurance that he would not stand in the way of a genuine effort to form a government. Norton at this stage asked that Costello be brought to give 'advice and help' to another meeting, limited to prospective ministers. On Saturday, 14 February the leaders met again in the Mansion House at 8 p.m.; present were Mulcahy, Costello, Dillon and the prospective ministers for Fine Gael, Clann na Talmhan and Clann na Poblachta. When the structure and personnel of party representation in the cabinet had been agreed, Costello was formally invited to become Taoiseach.

On the Friday evening Costello had been visiting with some of his closest legal and political colleagues. He told them that if a government was formed he would not be a minister and 'in no circumstances' would consent to be Attorney-General. He now faced the prospect of senior office with considerable reluctance. He discussed the implications with members of his family, old friends and, in particular, sought the advice of Dr. T. F. O'Higgins and Arthur Cox, the prominent Dublin solicitor. Unanimously they urged that he had no alternative but to accept. For him, as for the men who asked him to become Taoiseach, the choice was almost inevitable. At 9 o'clock on Sunday, 15 February 1948, Costello agreed to accept office.

Few other Fine Gael leaders could have hoped to win the support of Clann na Poblachta. Costello, over a period of years, had persuaded MacBride to exchange his extreme fringe republicanism for constitutional and parliamentary activity. Costello also had the advantage of close association with Tadhg Murphy of Labour (subsequently Minister for Local Government) and, through his own father, an old association with the Larkin family. Although never a minister, he had a background of experience in government, including a period of intense representation of Irish interests in the Commonwealth conferences. Costello was noted as a fair, impartial and skilful chairman. He had also been one of the earliest public advocates of a coalition alternative to unchanged single-party rule; as early as 1944 he asserted that 'in all democratic nations the historic answer to a national emergency is coalition government.' (*Irish Press*, 24 May 1944.)

Initially, Costello had very little opportunity to be more than chairman. Even before he took office, his hands were tied by inter-party agreements. The National Labour group's support was critical for the embryonic government and it was known that they were under strong internal and external pressure to support Fianna Fáil. The main issue troubling National Labour was their claim to direct representation at the International Labour Conference at Geneva, up to then secured by Larkin's Workers' Union of Ireland. Approached by Everett on this issue, Costello was unable to give any undertaking; he could only promise that if an inter-party government was formed National Labour would get 'a square deal.' The incident is indicative of Costello's narrow range of influence as Taoiseach during the first inter-party period. The original allocation of state departments had been arranged between the parties before his own selection and the subsequent behaviour of the parties showed no willingness to extend his rights as leader.

So, when the Labour-nominated Minister for Local Government died, the post was taken over for a week by the party leader, Norton, until the Parliamentary Labour Party met and nominated Michael Keyes as successor; Costello nominated Keyes on the following day. Similarly, it was noted that in the absence of the Minister for External Affairs, MacBride's position was assumed by the only other Clann na Poblachta minister, Dr. Noel Browne, although he was one of the most junior members of the cabinet. The only senior governmental appointment actually made by Costello was that of Cecil Lavery as Attorney-General. Otherwise he was deprived by the circumstances of the customary patronage available to a Taoiseach. Even the eleven nominations to the Senate constitutionally accorded to the Taoiseach were in fact allocated to party leaders in accordance with their strength in the Dáil.

Professor Chubb's account gives some further indications that the Taoiseach's powers were considerably reduced in this period :

> though the price of the continuation of a wide coalition such as the 'inter-party' government was substantial forbearance and a considerable freedom for each minister in his own sphere, a few ministers in the 1948-51 government would not pay the price. Some made policy statements which, when called into question, were said to be personal opinions. One minister attacked the Labour Court at the very time when his colleague, the Minister for Industry and Commerce, was considering trade union representations about it. The Minister for External Affairs expressed views on financial policy which were well-known to be contrary to those of the Minister for Finance. It became clear that 'inter-party' cabinet discipline was loose. The leaders of the various parties insisted on voicing their sometimes dissimilar views and defending their sometimes inconsistent conduct. The Minister for Finance was prepared to argue in the Dáil for the widest latitude : 'Have we got to the stage,' he asked, 'when men, just because they join the government circle, must all, as one deputy said, when they go out of the council chamber, speak the same language?'[1]

There is also some evidence that in this first period of inter-party government some senior civil servants, as well as ministers, were prepared to ignore the normal usages of ministerial and collective responsibility. MacBride's own interest in an extensive reforestation programme, for instance, led to a curious incident in which senior governmental officials attempted to cut across his own personal negotiations with a foreign diplomat to promote the policy by making a tree-planting programme a pre-requisite for Marshall Aid. There was also a confrontation, again involving MacBride and senior officers of the Department of Finance, at the time of devaluation. Another incident, this time involving Norton and the Secretary of the Department of Social Welfare, led to the dismissal of the latter; in response to a Private Notice Question from the Leader of the Opposition, Costello spelled out the theory of ministerial control of the civil service and gave the full correspondence relating to the case.[2]

Perhaps even more significant in the development of the relations of Taoiseach and cabinet, and in the history of this first inter-party government, was a major departure from usual administrative convention. For the first time since the foundation of the state, there was no member of the cabinet secretariat present at government meetings. The situation developed because of MacBride's conviction that after eleven years in office under de Valera, the Secretary of the Department of the Taoiseach, who is also Secretary to the government, should not be privy to the new cabinet's discussions. It was a far cry from the Cosgrave decade when Diarmuid Ó hEigeartaigh remained at the cabinet table for all discussions, party political as well as governmental. Instead the Chief Whip took notes at the meetings and the subsequent minutes and decisions were drafted and circulated by the cabinet secretariat in the usual way. There can be no doubt that this departure from established procedure weakened both Taoiseach and cabinet and contributed to the breakdown of internal communication which was a feature of the last days of this government. The fact that not all decisions were fully and accurately recorded was a factor in the 'Mother and

46

Child' controversy. It has also led to the suggestion that perhaps the most important acts of the 1948-51 government, the repeal of the External Relations Act and the declaration of the Republic, were Costello's own personal decision. The allegation was made by Lemass in the Dáil in 1948 and has been frequently repeated; as late as 1960 the Irish correspondent of *The Round Table* could speak of the 'petulant personal decision which severed our attenuated connexion with the Commonwealth.'[3] This version of events is connected to a suggestion that Costello took umbrage at a formal reception by the Governor-General of Canada and reacted by announcing that Ireland was leaving the Commonwealth. Fortunately Costello's own memorandum on the circumstances surrounding both the decision and its announcement can be quoted *in extenso* :

On the 6 August 1948 Mr. de Valera, then Leader of the Opposition, initiated the debate on the Adjournment of the Dáil, and a considerable part of his speech was concerned with considering the relationship which then existed between this country and the States of the British Commonwealth, and he outlined his views and opinions as to our international status and the effect of the External Relations Act of 1936. In the course of his reply the then Tánaiste, Mr. William Norton, dealt with some of Mr. de Valera's views, and referred in some detail to the views which he had expressed during the debate in the Dáil on that Act. Mr. Norton said (Col. 2440/1 *Dáil Debates,* Vol. 112, 6 August 1948) :

'I said it then and I repeat it again now, I say now that I think it would do our national self-respect good both at home and abroad if we were to proceed without delay to abolish the External Relations Act.'

Mr. de Valera then said (Col. 2441) 'go ahead.' Mr. Norton said : 'That was my view then on the position as I saw it. That is my view today.' Mr. de Valera then said : 'You will get no opposition from us.'

47

Deputy Peadar Cowan, at Cols. 2451 *et seq.*, expressed the strong view that the External Relations Act 1936 should be repealed.

Deputy Michael J. O'Higgins dealt with the matter (Col. 2458 *et seq.*) and expressed the wish at Col. 2462 that 'some firm declaration as to what is the intention of the government regarding this whole matter' should be made by the Minister for External Affairs, Mr. Seán MacBride.

These matters so raised on the Adjournment appeared to me to make it a matter of urgency for the government to make up its mind as to its attitude on the External Relations Act of 1936. I accordingly on my own motion raised the matter with the government. My clear view was that a decision to repeal it should be taken by the government before they might appear to be forced to do so by, for example, the introduction of a private member's Bill in the Dáil to repeal the Act. I had myself arrived firmly at the conviction that it was nationally desirable that the Act should be repealed. I was not, as has been frequently suggested, influenced by or subjected to any pressure by Mr. MacBride or any of his followers. I was sincerely convinced that it was very desirable that, as I subsequently explained in the Dáil in introducing the Bill to repeal the Act, there should be an end to the situation where Irishmen were killing Irishmen and that the gun should be taken out of Irish politics. The repeal of the Act, I felt, would contribute greatly to that objective. I believe our hopes were achieved.

An express decision was taken by the government that the External Relations Act should be repealed and the necessary legislation introduced immediately the Dáil reassembled.

It is necessary to emphasise that this was an express government decision, unanimously taken, before I had finally drafted my speech on 'Ireland in International

Affairs' and before I left for Canada. Following normal procedure the intention was to introduce the necessary Bill in the Dáil after the Recess.

I cannot say positively whether or not this decision is recorded in the Cabinet Minutes as at that time neither the Secretary nor Assistant Secretary of the Government attended Cabinet meetings. That the decision was definitely taken, I have no doubt. I was fully conscious of it when drafting the speech for the Canadian Bar Association and particularly during my various interviews with representatives of Irish American organisations whom I met in New York enroute to Canada.

If the memorandum is conclusive evidence that the decision was governmental (and it is borne out by other cabinet members of the period) it also makes clear Costello's readiness to act, in his own right, as spokesman for the government. While in Canada he was informed that the *Sunday Independent* had published an article announcing the government's intentions. Obviously he would be asked to comment on the report, but a telegram from MacBride in Dublin advised against any immediate public statement by the Taoiseach. MacBride was influenced in giving this advice by the presence in Dublin of Philip Noel-Baker, British Secretary of State for Commonwealth Relations, and by the knowledge that London had not adverted to the distinct change in Irish policy already indicated in Dáil statements and in the refusal to accept sealed letters of credence from a new Argentinean representative addressed to the King; this had been the standard form for accrediting diplomats up to that time and had been reluctantly accepted by de Valera. Faced with a dilemma, Costello's own view was that:

this advice, though well intentioned, was one that I felt I would not be permitted by my questioners in the Press Gallery of the House of Commons, Ottawa, to adopt. . . . Having given the matter the fullest possible consideration

49

I came to the conclusion that as the report was in fact true, and as the government intended to repeal the Act, there was nothing in honesty and decency open to me but to admit the truth. . . . The decision to do so was entirely my own and taken with a full sense of responsibility.[4]

In other matters he was not often free to exercise this full responsibility. In an effort to resolve some differences that arose, and possibly also to reduce both the length and asperity of cabinet meetings, Costello attempted to use cabinet committees to discuss the details of particular policy areas. The cabinet committee system has considerably increased the influence of the British Prime Minister. This Irish experiment was not a success. The committees barely functioned at all and the ministers still felt free to bring issues to the cabinet as a whole or directly to the Taoiseach. The experience of this period underscores the more general point that the Irish governmental system is sufficiently small and compact, the 'load' of policy decisions it carries sufficiently light, that it does not require an extensive network of committees. The Taoiseach and senior ministers are sufficiently accessible and junior ministers generally sufficiently visible to maintain control and effective communication. At the same time, the final act in the collapse of the first inter-party government revealed the dangers of allowing any laxity in the discipline of collective responsibility and the advantage of preserving established conventions and procedures.

The details of how the government came to an end scarcely belong to an essay on the role of the Taoiseach. However, there are elements in the situation which are directly relevant to the theme. In the first instance, it is now clear that to attribute the collapse simply to a policy disagreement on the 'Mother and Child' scheme, or to a climb-down in the face of ecclesiastical pressure, is far from a complete explanation. Much of the trouble arose from a developing personality clash within Clann na Poblachta involving MacBride, Browne and Noel Hartnett. MacBride gave his account in a statement to the Fifth Ard-Fheis of his party at the end of June 1951. In it he detailed the disintegration of their relationship:

> It was some time in the early part of 1950 that I began to notice a change in Dr. Browne's attitude. He tended to develop a dictatorial and domineering attitude and sought to create dissension on various issues, most of which were unimportant. . . . Finally last November I decided that I should have a frank discussion with Dr. Browne and should ensure that he understood fully the damage that would result from any internal dissension of this nature. In the course of this discussion he stated that he had been trying to pick an issue with me and would continue to do so until he succeeded. This was accompanied by a strong denunciation of the Standing Committee and of the Clann. Dr. Browne declared that he had no confidence in the Clann, that it was useless and that he was not prepared to 'waste his time in it'; that he would have resigned from the Government and the Clann some time previously were it not for the fact that he 'would regret it afterwards'. Finally, that he would seek an issue upon which to bring down the government, force a general election and break up the Clann.

Although MacBride alerted the chairman of the National Executive and Standing Committee on 11 November he apparently made no effort to keep his governmental colleagues in touch with these developments. By February 1951, Browne had threatened to resign and the disagreement was being publicised. MacBride's account in his speech continues:

> it became obvious that unless he resigned the Taoiseach would be forced to ask for his resignation. I considered that it would be undesirable to allow this to happen. Dr. Browne was a member of the government as my nominee on behalf of the Clann; it was clearly my responsibility to ask him to resign when it became clear that nothing further could be done to make him act responsibly. A most invidious

position would have arisen had the Taoiseach, who was a member of another party, requested his resignation on his own initiative. Dr. Browne was still a member of the Clann and I was still responsible for his presence in the cabinet. I could not even begin to justify his conduct or to stand over his actions; yet as the leader of the party I had to stand over him so long as he remained in the government as my nominee. In these circumstances a most difficult situation would have arisen had he been asked to resign by the Taoiseach. Accordingly, after very careful consideration, on 10 April, I wrote requesting Dr. Browne to tender his resignation to the Taoiseach.

Accepting this account, the question of whether MacBride usurped the Taoiseach's functions arises. His own argument is that Browne was not required to comply with the demand for resignation, in which event—as a dissident party member —MacBride would no longer have been responsible for him. On the other hand, it is clearly the right of the Taoiseach to demand the resignation of ministers and it might be argued that no letter should have been sent without Costello's prior approval. The point might further be made that in forcing Browne's resignation at this time MacBride was, in effect, deciding on a dissolution—again, a right of the Taoiseach. Perhaps a more serious practical question arises from MacBride's effort to cope with Browne as a party rather than a governmental matter. Arguably, he should have reported his conversation with Browne in November to Costello as Taoiseach; certainly that would have been expected in a single-party government. At the end, it was a senior member of the cabinet secretariat who invoked the regular processes of the governmental machine to prevent Browne from using the established communications network to publicise the disagreement prematurely.

It is noticeable that in the second inter-party period of government Costello was more firmly established and in control. He insisted that the Secretary attend the cabinet and take minutes of decisions; the official was only asked to withdraw while party political or electoral matters were discussed. With a much more confined grouping of parties and considerably enhanced political prestige it was easier for Costello to exert his influence as Taoiseach, although his own conviction on the character of the office remained closer to the limited views expressed in the 1937 constitutional debate than to the more extensive concept of prime ministerial power so evident in post-war Britain. It was this personal attitude towards the office as much as anything else that inhibited him in shaping the second inter-party cabinet. Inter-party considerations dictated Norton's right to claim Industry and Commerce; Costello's own political values prevented him from insisting, as he would have preferred, that McGilligan again accept the Department of Finance rather than become Attorney-General; and when T. F. O'Higgins made a claim on the Department of Health based upon family sentiment, Costello conceded the appointment.

The Taoiseach was conscious that some ministers had lost the freshness of their first term of office; both ministers and officials knew each other better and were less abrasively acting on each other to stimulate policy initiatives. Costello himself reached out to prod individual ministers or encourage particular projects. On at least one occasion this led the Fine Gael Minister for Finance, Gerard Sweetman, to complain of undue interference by the Taoiseach in internal departmental policy. It might also be noted that Costello appointed a parliamentary secretary who was electorally dependent on himself and had long experience as a senior civil servant in order to provide himself with a second governmental economic adviser.

Generally inclined, in common with other ministers of these periods, to emphasise the harmony and lack of major disagreement on policies (as against personalities), Costello still maintains his preference for the Taoiseach in a role as chairman rather than chief. The head of government, in his view today, should consult colleagues and, in the event of a major dispute, could always offer to resign as a way of exerting control. Given the discipline of Irish parties, he does not favour any frequent use of the free vote in the Dáil and is adamant that in both his periods of office the decision on parliamentary dissolution rested with him, as it should always lie with the Taoiseach.

NOTES: J. A. Costello

[1]Basil Chubb, *The Government,* Dublin 1968.
[2]*Dáil Debates,* 124/422-432, 21 February 1951.
[3]*Round Table,* vol. 50, March 1960, 185.
[4]For an account of the *Sunday Independent* Story see article by Hector Legge in *Sunday Independent,* 1 November 1970, p. 11.

5

Seán Lemass

Lemass entered office in 1959 as undisputed leader.
Although there was some press speculation regarding a
possible succession contest in Fianna Fáil and questions about
the acceptability of Lemass to some of the more doctrinaire
party supporters, there was no serious doubt about his claim.
De Valera had already named him heir apparent, not merely
by installing him as Tánaiste in 1945 but more recently in
speeches at the party's Ard Fheis. Lemass was recognised
as the most able and energetic of the ministers; he was also
the youngest member of the original de Valera cabinet of
1932—of whom three other members still remained in office
in 1959. He had been active for thirty years in the organisation of the party and it was Lemass, after the 1948 defeat,
who had accepted the task of restoring party morale.

Lemass saw that Fianna Fáil required a new, major programme of activity to survive loss of office. The impact of the
electoral defeat affected not only the ex-ministers but rank
and file parliamentary members, local representatives, party
officials and supporters up and down the country. All had
lost status; all had reduced access to where power and influence lay. Local standing required a nation-wide reorganisation. In the first instance, however, it demanded a vigorous
performance by the parliamentary party and its leaders.
Lemass shouldered the biggest burden of parliamentary
opposition for his party during the Inter-party period of office.
He replied to the Budget speech in both 1948 and 1949, spoke
on the vote for the Taoiseach's Department, the Social
Welfare Bill, and the Republic of Ireland Bill, as well as

being the most frequent and most effective Fianna Fáil contributor to topics more closely allied to his own area of interest and responsibility in Industry and Commerce. At the same time he became Managing Director of the *Irish Press* group and embarked on an expansionist policy there. Indeed his performance in the period 1948-51 underlined the accuracy of an observation attributed to a senior official, made to Costello when he first became Taoiseach, that the suggestion of one-man rule under de Valera should be discounted, that Lemass was 'the real dictator'.

Lemass has told Michael Mills:

As far as Fianna Fáil was concerned, there was a risk we fully recognised, that the great organisation which we had built up throughout the country would begin to disintegrate when it found the Party for the first time in Opposition. So, we embarked in a very vigorous reorganisation campaign in which members of the previous Government were free to participate; so that by 1951 we had a much more effective organisation than we had in 1948.

He himself concentrated on the Dáil and the press and was clearly dissatisfied with the effort made by some of his colleagues in grass-roots organisation. They may have been free to participate, in fact not that much was done. In the second period of Inter-party government, Lemass took direct charge of grass-roots reorganisation himself. He was installed as full-time, paid Director of Organisation of Fianna Fáil from 1954-57 and used the services of young bloods to prune some older growths within the party and replace some of the men he himself had introduced into positions of local leadership thirty years earlier when Fianna Fáil was being established. This ginger group included men destined for ministerial office later—Blaney, Haughey, Lenihan, Boland—and Senator Eoin Ryan. For the first time lists of party members at cumann level were drawn up, details and reports on local organisation amassed and a conscious effort made to prepare the party for the future. The campaign succeeded, as four successive general elections subsequently testified, but a price

56

was paid. The seeds of distrust were sown within the party; a gap developed between the old guard and many of the new men; and Lemass's own successful intrusion into local organisation was perhaps envied by the man who had largely claimed responsibility up to this, Gerry Boland.

Within government, when the party was in office, as de Valera's health and age reduced his efficiency, Lemass emerged progressively as the strong man. As his own powers extended, the Department of Industry and Commerce had become more and more an empire within the governmental and economic structure of Ireland. Stretching into all the main semi-state bodies, still retaining responsibilities that would be later hived-off to the separate Departments of Transport and Power, and of Labour, the office in Kildare Street became a breeding ground for the new generation of public servants strategically placed in other departments, governmental agencies and semi-state bodies.

Lemass by the late fifties had attained the reality of power; he was in the position to shape the main thrust of public policy. To some extent, the continuing occupation of the Taoiseach's office by de Valera was a political advantage, enabling Lemass to push through changes that were cloaked by the apparent changelessness of 'the Chief'. But there were disadvantages and frustrations in being executive officer rather than captain of the ship of state, especially when the executive wanted action and the captain favoured resting at anchor.

The tension between Lemass and de Valera, reflecting totally different attitudes towards governmental leadership, went back nearly a quarter of a century. An intense and unswerving loyalty bound the younger man to his leader; he recognised and respected in de Valera a capacity in the political sphere which he could describe as genius. But Lemass was often critical of de Valera's attitude towards governmental power. He was irritated, from the beginning, by his chief's tendency to back-off decision if argument developed. This did not, of course, apply to large political or constitutional issues but in the day-to-day routine of decision making, the automatic competition between departments for priority,

57

de Valera was slow to over-ride a protesting minister. De Valera sought unanimity; Lemass's whole instinct, by comparison, was for action. He recognised that the price of unity could easily become inaction; he believed that a Taoiseach's task was both to hold his team together and to press forward with an active, even controversial, programme.

Yet by 1959, on balance, Lemass had created a sufficiently effective and extensive power base for himself within the government, the administration and the party not to relish a change of status. Through the 'fifties, and more particularly from 1957 on, Lemass had almost the full powers of a Prime Minister. Economic issues had replaced the earlier purely political emphasis and the task of leading the new planning thrust in policy was largely left to Lemass. De Valera, by now, was much reduced in functional efficiency and initiative by age and blindness. Although ministers of the period reject the thesis that Lemass was in control from 1957-59—one put it firmly that 'Dev's was still the decisive voice'—he had achieved a nearly dominant influence. The continued presence of de Valera imposed little restraint on Lemass's aims and even provided a useful conservative cloak for a changing public policy.

Lemass's one doubt, shared with his other colleagues, was whether or not he could hope to match de Valera's established electoral appeal. No one yet knew—few were prepared to estimate—the likely effect of the change of leadership on Fianna Fáil fortunes. The party without de Valera was an almost alien concept; the image of strong personal leadership had frozen into accepted reality. There was no doubt that Lemass would be accepted by the party, though with long, lingering glances backwards, but would the voting public accept? Any reservations that Lemass entertained were stilled by those close to him politically, in particular by Dr. James Ryan. There remained only the residual reluctance to change the habits and life-style of a minister for the more sedate role still apparently demanded of a Taoiseach.

There was no reluctance to tackle the responsibility of office. Although now 60, Lemass moved like a young man in a hurry. Partly this was a conscious reaction to the style and tempo of de Valera's leadership, partly a response to new needs as government assumed ever greater responsibility for the management of the economy, partly a reflection of Lemass's attitude to decision-making. He did not believe in agonising before action and was not worried about the prospect of making mistakes. He told Michael Mills:

Generally I would agree that the quick decision is always better than the long delayed decision. My own personal experience was that once you had some clear concept of a problem that you rarely added to your wisdom by going back and looking at it again and again and again, delaying the decision. You are just as likely to make mistakes taking the proper decisions as taking the delayed decision, but at any rate you have a decision to work on. As long as you keep a certain flexibility of mind you can make adjustments. (*Irish Press,* 4 February 1969.)

The change of leadership scarcely involved any major policy changes; under Lemass there was an acceleration of existing developments rather than any radical new departures. But in the matter of forming an administration he was conscious of the need to establish a generational change; he might have envied and echoed the words of John F. Kennedy's inaugural that a torch had been passed on to a new generation of leaders. He was certainly determined not to allow himself to follow de Valera's example and be trapped by the past. Indeed, it is important to recognise the extent to which Lemass as Taoiseach was consciously reacting to his own observations and experience of de Valera in office. But at the beginning, there were few changes in the first Lemass administration, it remained set in the mould created by de Valera in 1932. The details are evident in the tables published in the appendix giving the composition of Irish cabinets.

Lemass's recollection of how he approached the formation of his first cabinet and his reflections on the selection of ministers provide an illuminating comment on the central theme of the relations of Taoiseach and cabinet:

I considered whether I should make Jim Ryan Tánaiste, not because of any personal consideration but because I felt that, in the government as it is, the seniority of the Minister for Finance should be marked in some way. In effect he does sit at the cabinet table in a much stronger position to criticise or to veto proposals of other ministers than even the Taoiseach because every proposal involves finance of some kind. Therefore, his position is quite powerful in the government and I felt that the fact that the Minister for Finance was a little senior to the other ministers should be indicated by the fact that he was appointed Tánaiste, and that he should automatically be Tánaiste. In fact the Tánaiste's only function is to take the chair at cabinet meetings when the Taoiseach is absent.

MacEntee was the senior minister. It would have seemed a rebuke to him if I did not appoint him as Tánaiste so I did appoint him. I suppose Jack Lynch, by appointing Frank Aiken as Tánaiste, is also accepting seniority as the basis for the position rather than the functions to be discharged. That will be a problem for Jack Lynch when Frank Aiken retires because I think he may be reluctant to accept seniority. It is far more important however to maintain goodwill and harmony than seek a more effective distribution of responsibility.

The young men were Boland, Hillery, Blaney and Jack Lynch in the early stages. It would be a good thing for the government if there were some device by which the opportunity of appointing new men to the cabinet presented itself fairly regularly. This raises the question of the age at which a minister should retire. One of the weaknesses in the cabinet here is that most of its members depend upon their jobs for their livelihood. It is serious for them if they find themselves out of a job. In Britain this problem does not arise; they can give retired ministers posts like that of colonial governor, which gives them income without cabinet membership and even an opportunity of a dignified retirement which could, in some circumstances, be called promotion. We do not have that here.

My view as to the capabilities of individual members of the government would be a personal view but I would certainly have no difficulty in putting them in order of merit and it would be helpful from the point of view of the party if one could be sure of the opportunity of doing this. Young men are coming along in the party now and their mind is set on when they will reach the stage of being in line for consideration for a ministerial appointment. They will feel frustrated if they see men remaining in office whom they feel are less competent than themselves or so old they should be retired. I did not get an opportunity to make any changes at all until 1961. I made changes then, and would have kept on making changes time and again—if for no other reason than to make it quite clear to any new man that if he showed he had ability the road to promotion was fairly open to him.

In fact, Lemass made two changes prior to the 1961 General Election. Just one month after he assumed office, he moved Moran from the Department of the Gaeltacht to the Department of Lands and promoted Gerald Bartley from Parliamentary Secretary to be Minister for the Gaeltacht. Incidentally it should be noted that Lemass has expressed considerable reservations about the conventional use of the parliamentary secretaryship as an automatic route of entry to ministerial office. The appointment of Bartley came as news to the cabinet and the party. Lemass did not discuss this, nor indeed any subsequent, ministerial appointment with his cabinet.

Lemass took the view that the selection of ministers was a matter for the Taoiseach—not for general governmental decision. He appears to have been more ready to sound opinion among trusted colleagues than de Valera had been. In particular, Lemass consulted Ryan as a senior and experienced minister whose advice and information he could evaluate as entirely disinterested. This is not to say that Ryan's advice was automatically followed. The final choice of ministers and portfolios, in Lemass's view, lay with the

61

Taoiseach—to allow it to go to the cabinet would be to abdicate.

The second governmental change made by Lemass before 1961 was occasioned by a request from Oscar Traynor, whose health was failing, for assistance in the Department of Justice. Specifically he asked for a parliamentary secretary who could accept responsibility for a much needed programme of law reform. The first name suggested was that of Seán Flanagan —backed apparently by both Lemass and Traynor. But the cabinet on this occasion dissuaded the Taoiseach and insisted that the parliamentary secretaryship (and implicitly an early ministerial appointment) should go to C. J. Haughey. It is difficult to know to what extent Lemass was here seeking to avoid any change of nepotism (certainly his judgement must have been affected by the fact that Haughey was his son-in-law), or whether he was exhibiting that reserved ambiguity about Haughey in politics that was to emerge again when the question of his own succession emerged. In the event, in May 1960, according to Lemass's own account he called in Haughey and told him that it was his duty as Taoiseach to convey the government's invitation to become a parliamentary secretary and his duty as a father-in-law to advise him not to be fool enough to take it.

As already indicated above Lemass determined to assert a more influential voice for the Taoiseach in naming not only ministers but also parliamentary secretaries. When forming his government in 1961 he called people in to tell them that he wanted them in this junior governmental role but could not guarantee that they would be appointed; that decision still lay with the cabinet. There is no evidence that Lemass did not get his way in 1961, although the fact that only three parliamentary secretaries were named, that only two of these were new men and that Flanagan's name was not included is suggestive. It is evident that while O'Malley was given a free hand in the Board of Works—long recognised as a virtually independent sub-department of Finance—Lenihan encountered difficulties with Moran in the Department of Lands, where he had been informally allocated responsibility for fisheries.

It was Lemass's aim and intention to give the parliamentary secretary a defined function and responsibility : to make him a junior minister of the government rather than an assistant to a particular minister. Possibly he also intended to use the younger men's initiative as a prod for less active ministers. It is known that there was at least one considerable clash between a minister and his parliamentary secretary under Lemass in which the junior man leaned on his understanding with the Taoiseach to claim access to the cabinet and the senior man insisted on his legal prerogatives. A correspondence followed, in the course of which the Civil Service advisers pressed the point that the parliamentary secretary's case had no standing under the Ministers and Secretaries Act. In the event, what might have proved a difficult, but revealing, clash was forestalled by the 1965 General Election. Following the poll, Lemass, without consulting the cabinet, chose and named six new parliamentary secretaries, four of whom subsequently became ministers.

Lemass also used the occasion to arrange for the political retirement of both MacEntee and Bartley, and to reshuffle his cabinet. Since the thirties, when MacEntee had served as a very orthodox Minister for Finance, there had been an area of tension and disagreement between Lemass and himself. It was a matter of temperament but also reflected a difference in approach to government between the two men illustrated in an incident in which Lemass—without reference to MacEntee (who was shadow Minister for Finance)—promised an arbitration scheme to a civil service delegation. MacEntee, in office, insisted on establishing a formal Commission on the subject. Although Lemass considered him better suited to Health than Finance he cannot have relished MacEntee's continuous wrangle with the medical profession, nor his old-established (and, to Lemass, undesirable) habit of writing letters to the newspapers. Lemass may well have thought MacEntee too inclined to accept a departmental view— whether in Finance or Health. There was the additional problem that in his Dublin constituency MacEntee had a well-organised machine with a highly experienced agent, both reluctant to see their man out of office or out of the Dáil. The result was a much publicised effort to restrain Lemass, culminating in a meeting of the parliamentary party at which MacEntee launched a direct attack on his Taoiseach. It was a nuisance, but ineffective; to be brushed aside by Lemass almost in Macmillan's phrase about 'a little local difficulty'.

Lemass depended on the old bonds of comradeship to exert his authority in dropping ministers. He recognised that this would not be possible in the future, and was also conscious that the single-transferable-vote system of election could give an established minister a significant power base. A man might threaten to bring 'a pal or two' into the division lobbies and bring down the government.

Yet he was insistent that ministers must function properly as decision-makers if the whole business of government was not to slow down. He himself was inclined to exert more control than de Valera; he knew the dangers of individual departments beginning semi-independent empires. Lemass saw his own function as Taoiseach as ensuring a balance within government and preventing unnecessary conflicts of policy. Apparently this was not generally a serious problem. But clearly more is involved in the role of Taoiseach than politic ways and gentle persuasions. On the vital issue of controlling possible dissident ministers, Lemass recognised that it might be necessary to exert the authority of office. A Taoiseach has to retain the right to remove ministers. To change government policy because of a threat of resignation would make the Taoiseach dependent on the minister. Lemass told his cabinet that if anyone resigned, the resignation would be accepted—though not necessarily on the spot. On one or two occasions he told a minister who said he was resigning to think it over for a week-end and then offer it again.

Lemass has also answered the question of what might happen where the personal opinion of the Taoiseach differed from that of the majority of his ministers. He told Michael Mills:

If the question was important enough then this would create a situation of cabinet crisis. This didn't happen in my case but one can see a point of time where a Taoiseach who felt strongly upon some major issue and realising that he could not bring the majority of his colleagues with him would have to say—'do as I do or get another Taoiseach'. This is the ultimate way in which a Taoiseach might exercise the authority of his office but this would happen very rarely and, of course, only on very major issues.

(*Irish Press,* 3 February 1969.)

In practice, Lemass did have some trouble with individual ministers. The most noted case was the resignation of Smith from Agriculture in October 1964. Smith, too, was an inheritance from the de Valera era. He had been appointed Parliamentary Secretary to the Taoiseach in the governmental reorganisation in September 1939 and entered the cabinet as Minister for Agriculture in January 1947 (in the governmental reshuffle following the establishment of the Department of Health and Social Welfare). Smith was among the Fianna Fáil leaders who took the view during the Inter-party periods that active opposition was unnecessary : that the 'Coalition' would fall apart of its own accord. This was not a view to which Lemass subscribed. In the Irish system the Department of Industry and Commerce and the Department of Agriculture are commonly engaged in a competition that reflects two basic economic interests and undoubtedly Lemass found Smith a less acceptable and reasonable cabinet colleague in the office than Ryan had been. When Lemass became Taoiseach he retained Smith and deferred some earlier resignation offers. By 1964 Smith's performance as minister was apparently more bother than it was worth to Lemass. Smith objected that efforts to settle an eight-week long building strike indicated a willingness to sacrifice rural to urban interests. He proffered his resignation and it was accepted. This was the first time that a Fianna Fáil minister had ever persisted in resigning on a question of policy. Smith spelled out his reasons in a letter of resignation published in the press, 7 October 1964 :

65

I have been thinking long and seriously since our meeting yesterday on what my future course of action should be and it appears as if there is nothing left for me to do but let you have, as I do now, my resignation as a member of the Government.

It is not necessary to go into any great detail on my reasons for taking this action since these have been repeatedly stated and discussed at one time or another at Government level. We all, I know, at one time or another made some effort to resist tyranny in all its forms, but when we are faced, as we are now, with not only a tyranny but a dishonest, incompetent one, matters become much more serious for the country. I say dishonest because of the utter disregard by the unions and their alleged leaders of the National Wage Agreement, entered into freely and generously, a few months ago, supposed to last for a period of two and a half years; incompetent because of the complete indiscipline of their union members and their own utter lack of leadership. Making agreements with such is a fraud. If proposals for such are recommended by the leaders, it is always a certainty that they will be rejected. If they are approved they are too weak even to try to enforce them. Those so-called leaders of the trade union movement whom our Minister for Industry and Commerce have (*sic*) been chasing around for years now could not lead their grand-mothers, if alive, as members of their respective unions.

They can be quite glib on the rising cost of living, profits and price control, and at the same time with their tongue in their cheek and being really led from the rear, make demands that they know when conceded can have only one result—rising costs and so on.

This is not legitimate trade unionism—it is tyranny and I refuse to prepare myself to live with it and accept it. Our people can be led to fight this plague even if we have to suffer. When reason and decency is abandoned there are only two courses—fight or surrender. I believe a stand like this will be in the interest of all in the end and I feel sure thousands of others are with me in this—even real trade union leaders should. There weren't too many clamouring for a 40-hour week in 1957 when we came into office. Workers could think of that with advantage to themselves. I am very sorry that I should feel obliged to take this course after all these years but you may rest assured I have not done so lightly but as the only course available having proper regard to the views I hold.

Yours sincerely,

P. J. SMITH, Minister for Agriculture.

Lemass apparently received news of this resignation before the formal letter reached him. Smith's effort to capture the headlines with a press conference were capped by Lemass's swift reaction in nominating Haughey to Agriculture. Although there was press speculation that Smith's departure would be a 'severe blow' to the government, the only threat was the possibility that by resigning his seat Smith might precipitate a general election. Within the party, the resignation caused no stir. In the country at large the promotion of Haughey, a city man, to head Agriculture became the main talking point. Lemass published a formal letter of acceptance:

Dear Paddy,

I have received your communication of yesterday informing me that your decision to resign from the government is irrevocable. I understand that you have already communicated this decision to the press.

In the circumstances I have no alternative but to accept the position. I regret the termination of our long and fruitful association in the Government, and I know that this regret will be shared by all your former colleagues. I wish you personally every good fortune in the future.

Yours sincerely,

SEÁN F. LEMASS.

By this time, of course, Lemass was ready to put his own stamp on the cabinet. He had already advised his new mini-

F

sters to establish their own reputations, had actively encouraged them to compete. In part, this was a reaction to the long period of one-man dominance under de Valera; in part, an essential contribution to Lemass's plan for a galvanised Civil Service machine with departments operating as 'developmental corporations'; in part a deliberate effort to stimulate a degree of professional competition. On occasions, it seemed, individual ministers went too far with public announcements of new policy departures not fully sanctioned by the cabinet.

In the process of image-building the younger ministers were ready to exploit the resources of the mass media and, it might be argued, were largely responsible for a new style of political comment in the press. The traditional, rather dull and frequently oblique columns of the lobby correspondents began to give way to 'colour' stories reporting Dáil sessions and to comment that centred on personalities. At its best, this could give a new and exciting air of freshness to the political scene. It could also, as critics pointed out, lead to calculated leaks and dramatic posturing for effect. In particular, it is alleged, the late Donogh O'Malley (both in the Department of Health and of Education) 'leapfrogged' the claims of other departments by public statements committing the government to new, and expensive, schemes. Probably the most striking example was his announcement of the 'free secondary education' scheme on 10 September 1966.

In July of that year Dr. P. J. Hillery was moved from Education to the new Department of Labour, and O'Malley succeeded to the post. The Department of Education had been undergoing a quiet revolution in the sixties under Lynch, Hillery and Colley. Lemass was sufficiently interested himself to intervene when changes were resisted by the Department of Finance and, to some extent, short-circuited full cabinet discussions. He had taken care to consult Dr. Ryan and make him party to the educational reconstruction programme that was evolving. O'Malley was looking for a programme of action and found one in a rough draft scheme for an extended free scheme of comprehensive post-primary education. The costs involved (given that no compensation was involved for the capital expenditure already made by the secondary schools) were not excessive. O'Malley discussed the possibilities of adoption with some close cabinet colleagues, but did not begin the rather lengthy process of having it raised at the cabinet. Instead, he chose the occasion of his maiden speech as minister to the National Union of Journalists, to announce:

> I propose from the coming school year, beginning in September of next year, to introduce a scheme whereby, up to the completion of the Intermediate Certificate course, the opportunity for free post-primary education will be available to all families.

The response was immediate and enthusiastic. Any qualifications about the scheme were brushed aside and a major (and apparently not fully planned) change in Irish education was launched. It is one of the most curious episodes in recent Irish politics, flying in the face of all conventional decision-making processes. The immediately involved interests—the secondary schools—were not consulted, governmental approval was not secured and the Minister for Finance was not consulted. The result was a private reprimand for O'Malley at the cabinet meeting of the following Tuesday, after a severe attack on the breach of collective responsibility made by the Minister for Finance, Lynch, who had not been in the country when the announcement was made. O'Malley's effort to involve the Taoiseach's authority was not entertained and he was instructed never to indulge in such public commitments of expenditure without previous governmental approval. But one is bound to ask how seriously the reprimand was intended given that the Taoiseach had reportedly both seen and amended the text of the speech prior to delivery. If a minister was here in breach of the doctrine of collective responsibility, then it must be said that the head of government shares some of the responsibility. Even though Lemass has denied seeing the speech it is significant that five members of his cabinet have separately

69

told the present author that they believed he had seen and amended it. This belief is likely to have affected their own behaviour. Certainly a number of them became conscious of O'Malley's determination to press his own political claims.

It might be argued that O'Malley was only doing what Lemass himself had preached and practised—the technique of mobilising popular support as a means of accelerating executive action. The Taoiseach regarded this as:

> part of the art of political leadership. One of the methods by which a head of a party or the head of a government leads his party along a political line of action is to speak in public in favour of a line of action before the government or the party had decided on it. This is a technique very frequently used and, of course, the Taoiseach or leader of a party who did this on a line which was bound to bring him into conflict with the party would be very foolish. But there are many cases where you could not get the decision in principle to proceed in a particular line taken in reasonable time without in some way committing your colleagues to following the line.
>
> (*Irish Press*, 3 February 1969.)

On occasions Lemass went far beyond this procedure. He was capable of flying balloons—through asides in his own or in other minister's speeches—and organising and inspiring press speculation on topics of concern. It might be going too far to speak of press manipulation but there can be no doubt that in the period journalists were used by the Taoiseach as well as by individual members of his cabinet.

Senior party critics of Lemass as Taoiseach have argued that far from giving his ministers more freedom than de Valera had allowed, he in fact was more inclined to interfere in the detailed work of departments. They have gone on to suggest that his desire to retain executive control in economic affairs in particular reduced his capacity to control and unify the whole apparatus of government. Certainly Lemass's own attitude towards the rationalisation of governmental function and the delegation of authority appears somewhat ambivalent. Whatever about his conscious desire to encourage ministerial initiative and enterprise, it is clear that his tendency to divert decisions to cabinet committees and his regular phone calls to ministers probing for action, tended to strengthen his own control *vis-à-vis* some individual ministers. At least one new entrant to the cabinet in 1965 has commented that by the time the younger men arrived Lemass was so senior and so experienced that they were ready to defer to him. On the other hand, more senior ministers report that Lemass left them alone to get on with their jobs.

In cabinet, Lemass was more ready than de Valera to press for a decision openly and to come down earlier than his predecessor on one side of an argument; he was not averse to votes in cabinet, or at party meetings. Again, critics and colleagues more enamoured of the de Valera mode of leadership have argued that this marked a weakening in governmental control, that issues were not discussed with the same thoroughness and completeness, that decisions were made, in the expressive phrase of one colleague, 'on the nod'. Another minister with experience under both men has pointed out that both the number and length of cabinet meetings declined under Lemass and there can be little doubt that there was a willingness to short-cut procedures.

Did this mean a decline in the Taoiseach's control? Critics say yes. But two other comments might be made. First, that Lemass did not permit adverse votes on major topics of significance to his own programmes—he did not require unanimity but did demand acquiescence. Second, against the charge that by cutting short discussion he created the seeds of disunity, must be set the fact that he recognised that extended policy debate itself could become divisive:

I, as Taoiseach in the cabinet, would sense the moment when there was a majority view formed in favour of a particular course; then I got that majority view recorded. Dev always worked for unanimity so he always let the argument go on, which was often a futile course because

71

the more you argued the more convinced you became of the rectitude of your own position and how wrong the other fellow was.

An example of Lemass's performance was the decision to send Irish troops to the Congo; this was the first occasion when Irish troops would be committed directly under the command of the United Nations, although earlier officers had been sent as UN observers to the Middle East. There was disagreement among senior ministers. MacEntee argued that Lumumba was a communist and that Ireland would be coming in on the wrong side; Aiken had reservations about sending troops and the Department of Finance questioned a proposal that might lead to increased costs. However, Lemass had made up his mind, there was a majority in the cabinet and he was quite willing to sanction the operation despite these objections.

Finally, in considering Lemass's relations with the cabinet, comes the question of his resignation. This was undoubtedly a political decision, calculated to allow Fianna Fáil to surmount a short-term economic problem and leaving enough time for the new incumbent to establish himself before the next general election. However, it has been suggested that by announcing his intention to retire in advance he considerably reduced his own influence on the choice of successor. On the other hand, there is some reason to doubt the extent to which Lemass actively sought to decide the succession. It is known that he contrived and initiated much of the press speculation on candidates during 1966 and that he 'encouraged' George Colley to think of himself as a potential Taoiseach and advised him to act accordingly. This is not to say that he actively worked for and backed Colley. Undoubtedly, too, he had reservations about Haughey's suitability for the top post in government. It may be that Lemass simply believed that it was desirable that there should be some contest for the leadership; this would make sense in a man who had a general belief in the efficacy of competition. It is certain that when the news of his imminent retirement broke, Lemass sent for Colley to return from a ministerial visit to the United States. It is also clear that when Lynch emerged as an acceptable leader within the party Lemass tried to persuade the other contenders to withdraw. But it is still too early to offer any final verdict on these events, except perhaps to register the point that the power and influence of a Taoiseach will tend to wane very rapidly once he is seen to be relinquishing office, and to suggest that in the end Lemass resigned several months earlier than he had originally intended.

6

Jack Lynch

Jack Lynch was the first Irish head of government to reach office after a contested internal party election: the first to face a cabinet which numbered men who had openly challenged his claim to leadership. A late arrival in the open contest for the succession in Fianna Fáil, he was type-cast by many observers as a compromise choice brought in to resolve a dilemma. In fact he had always been widely accepted within the party and at least one of his subsequent rivals had been prepared to back him originally for the leadership. Lynch's promotional career within government, the steady climb from Parliamentary Secretary through successively senior departments, also indicated the continuous approval and support of both de Valera and Lemass. Nevertheless the fact that there had been a competition for power, that camps had been formed and distinct loyalties declared within the Fianna Fáil parliamentary party ushered in a new period in Irish politics and government.

A Taoiseach who succeeds without a general election has only limited influence. He cannot hope to make his mark on the cabinet immediately and the initial Lynch cabinet registered only minimal changes from the last Lemass administration; indeed a minister who has served under both leaders registered the criticism that Lemass, by recruiting so many younger men into his cabinet, left Lynch little room for manoeuvre but another colleague countered by pointing out that Lemass could scarcely have been expected to keep offices open and the previous Taoiseach had managed the more difficult task of moving the older men from office. All the candidates in the succession contest were located in senior offices in Lynch's first cabinet: Haughey was moved to Finance and was replaced in Agriculture by Blaney and Colley left in Industry and Commerce. Lynch told the Dáil that he 'was not Taoiseach in a caretaker capacity' and settled down to the task of consolidating his political position.

Lynch's main strength was marked in an early series of by-election victories. Within a month of taking office he chalked up two seats for his party in Waterford and Kerry on 7 December 1966 and followed this with two more successes in Cork City and West Limerick the following November. He thus secured an over-all majority of four seats in the Dáil, all incidentally in Munster. He also indicated what was to become a major element in his future electoral strategy—a concentration on Labour as the main threat to Fianna Fáil support.

Despite his performance at the polls, Lynch appeared an inert governmental leader. It is known that he indicated to members of his cabinet that he did not approve of the emphasis on personal public relations which had been such a marked feature of the Lemass years. Lynch preferred the concept of the cabinet as a team to the more brilliant solo runs favoured by Lemass. But he was also conscious of the strength of the men about him and (perhaps unduly) impressed by the organisational talents of some party managers. He determined to stop up the flow of cabinet leaks that had enlivened Irish political journalism and comment in the fifties; he could not totally discipline men accustomed to public 'strokes' but insisted at least on a fuller discussion of issues before proposals were publicised.

The result was a change in the pace of government. Instant decision was replaced by longer periods of gestation. Especially in the early years there was an attempted renewed emphasis not only on proper cabinet procedures but on governmental involvement in departmental policies. Lynch made it clear that he expected ministers to take an interest in, and responsibility for, cabinet decisions beyond the range of their own departmental functions and political ambitions. There seems good reason to suppose that his efforts were not entirely successful.

Lynch was not that much senior in either age or governmental experience to the more ambitious men in his cabinet. He could not claim any long family connection in Fianna Fáil. He stressed the point years later in explaining his delay in demanding the resignations of Haughey and Blaney:

I think it is not unreasonable that I thought long and considered much the action I was to take.

Deputy Blaney came into this House in the same year as I did. With Deputy Boland, we received our seals of office on the same day 13 years ago from An tUachtarán. We had grown to political maturity together.

Deputy Haughey became a minister some few years later. The four of us were close as far as harmony in administration was concerned. Each one of us, in our different ministries, in our own way, desired to serve the country in the most efficient way we knew. Certainly, it was for me a sad day when our ministerial paths had to part. All three of them had long family traditions—as we have heard. . . . It made the task all the less easy that I realised that my family had not the same tradition of service or of membership of the Fianna Fáil party and that I was asking these two men to resign and that Deputy Kevin Boland resigned because he objected to my handling of the affair, obviously. This did not ease the heartbreak of my decision. I knew the effect it was likely to have on the political future of able and brilliant men.

(*Dáil Debates* 246/1336-7, 9 May 1970.)

It seems clear that in the years immediately preceding the crisis similar reservations affected the relationship of Taoiseach and cabinet. Some ministers pursued policies within their departments with little regard to the measured advice of their civil servants. It is doubtful if the doctrine of collective responsibility imposed any marked brake on their initiatives. Certainly they managed to capture headlines and public attention more readily than the Taoiseach.

76

Lynch seemed cast in the role of a pale and patient captain of a team whose stars were eager for applause but indifferent to discipline. In 1968 a contributor to *Hibernia* commented:

But then Jack Lynch has never been tested. Somebody described the present government as a coalition—a coalition between various strong-headed ministers each bent on the achievement of particular ambitions. Lynch is the mediator among them, and so far he has given them their head to an unusual degree. He let Boland blunder ahead with the referendum. He allowed Blaney, unchecked, to be ensnared by the farmers. He sanctioned Mickey Moran's mad plan to send the Civil Service to Castlebar.
None of these decisions are associated personally with Jack Lynch. This is the passive approach to leadership, and the natural corollary is that ministers supply the initiative.

While much of this seems justified, and provided ample opportunity for Opposition attacks, in the Dáil Lynch was willing to accept full responsibility; he took particular trouble to stress this after the failure of the referendum campaign:

I want to say with regard to references which have been made about my responsibility as head of government that it would have been an easy thing for me to lay about me after the referendum and try to deny my responsibility for the referendum results by rolling a few heads around the cabinet table. If and when there are to be changes in the government they will be of my own choosing. I will not be stampeded into this either by Opposition jibes here or by writers outside. So also will be the timing of the next election. The timing of the next election will also be of my choosing and I will, as any worthwhile politician would, choose the best time for it.

(*Dáil Debates* 236/2505-6, 7 November 1968.)

Yet Lynch still had not imposed his leadership on the cabinet team he had inherited from Lemass. However the general election campaign of 1969 showed that if Lynch lacked lustre, he did not lack electoral appeal. Party col-

77

leagues, political opponents and political observers alike recognised that if the re-drawing of the constituencies had provided the groundwork for a Fianna Fáil victory it was the Taoiseach's own tour of the country that secured the scale of the triumph.

There was little visible sign of change in either style or control when the new cabinet was named. Seniority remained the basic element in the selection of Childers to replace Aiken as Tánaiste, though the former's translation from the Department of Transport and Power to Health was a clear indication of approval and promotion. At the other end of the scale the movement of Flanagan from Health, which might have been seen as simply a way of providing Childers with a suitably demanding post of status, became an indication of demotion when his new post was named as Lands. With hindsight, it might be noted, as suggested earlier in this essay, that the low status in the ministerial hierarchy accorded to both Justice and Defence which was again reflected in the 1969 appointments, contained the seeds of the subsequent crisis in that they effectively reduced the flow of direct and accurate information on national security issues to the Taoiseach. However the real clue to Lynch's intentions might be seen in the reorganisation of ministries involving the careers of both Blaney and Boland. The former's translation from the prestigious, if difficult, Department of Agriculture to any new department must be seen as demotion for a senior man. Although the Taoiseach spoke about the significance of the new Department of Physical Planning, it could scarcely be compared in status to one of the oldest and most powerful departments of state. Moreover the proposed change also reduced Boland's Department of Local Government and the substitution of Social Welfare responsibility for this loss was little compensation.

One might still wonder that Lynch did not take stronger action against ministerial colleagues whose attitude towards his leadership remained, at best, ambiguous. The failure to act is particularly noticeable since Boland, who had been, in the words of a colleague, 'rumbling about resignation' since

Lemass's time, had again indicated a willingness to go to the backbenches. Indeed the Taoiseach took trouble to inform the Dáil of the fact in his closing remarks on the debate nominating members of the government after Boland had broken with convention and become the first ministerial nominee ever to speak on such a motion; Lynch, possibly preparing the ground for another resignation threat, pointed out :

> Let me say this. Deputy Kevin Boland said earlier he was not interested in office. He came to see me and said if I did not want him on the front bench he was quite happy to go to the back benches.
>
> *(Dáil Debates* 241/146, 2 July 1969.)

Undoubtedly an element in the decision not to dispense with these ministers was the recognition that no previous Taoiseach had ever openly showed his hand in exercising the constitutional right to dismiss or drop ministers; certainly no one of the stature of Blaney had ever been fired. There was no way of knowing the political cost of such an action and he had grounds for supposing it might be unacceptably high : it might cause trouble within the party, would probably be accompanied by Boland's resignation and would certainly be interpreted as giving way to pressure from the farming interests and the Opposition. Moreover Lynch was conscious of the work done by both Boland and Blaney for his party and of their positions as senior officers in the party.

In the event, of course, circumstances overtook political decision by the Taoiseach. The renewed outbreak of violence in Northern Ireland reintroduced into the internal politics of the state a highly emotive and uncontrollable factor. This essay is not the place to attempt any detailed analysis of precisely what occurred. The development of a coherent policy position towards Northern affairs itself involved a degree of strain that can be measured in part by a comparison of the Taoiseach's major statements on Northern affairs.

The essential point in regard to the role of the Taoiseach in these events is that the internal cabinet tensions, competitions and disagreements which it exposed were inherent in the governmental situation ever since Lynch assumed office. Despite repeated denials, there could be no doubt of the degree of rivalry within the cabinet. The events of August 1969 presented the occasion for the challenge to Lynch's leadership to assume a policy orientation. Blaney and Boland were identified as reluctant to accept all the implications of Lynch's increasingly insistent emphasis on a pacific policy; they saw it as a withdrawal from traditional Fianna Fáil 'republicanism'. The dispute was publicised following a speech by Blaney in Letterkenny in December. In public, it was reiterated, the speech did not deviate from government policy; nevertheless in a radio interview Lynch spoke of a private reprimand of Blaney, while the latter on the same programme was dismissive of the Taoiseach's criticism.

In 1970 repeated rumours of internal governmental division were accompanied by doubts that the administration was failing to act against illegal organisation operating in both parts of the country. Lynch suffering from 'extreme fatigue' was told by his medical advisers to reduce his work schedule at the beginning of February. The North continued to erupt. Then in rapid succession came the announcement of Ó Moráin's resignation, following immediately by the dismissal of Haughey and Blaney and the resignation of Boland and his Parliamentary Secretary, Paudge Brennan.

This whole episode and the subsequent debates of confidence in the Dáil, the arms trial and Public Accounts Committee hearings have given some new illumination to the relations of Taoiseach and cabinet. There are still considerable and irreconcilable conflicts in all the welter of evidence but a number of points emerge clearly.

One is that an Irish head of government has shown that not even a major cabinet and party crisis, involving the most senior members, can force out a man determined to retain the office of Taoiseach. Once in power, even if he is slow to use that power, a Taoiseach cannot be successfully challenged. Indeed, despite the initial indications of instability and publicised dissensions and opposition within the parliamentary party, it can be argued that the events of May 1970 actually strengthened Lynch's position both in government and in the Fianna Fáil party. He was able to dispense with four ministers from the de Valera and Lemass periods and replace them with men of his own choice. It has been suggested that the new ministers were all 'Colley men' but the observation, even if accurate, misses the point that they owe their posts to Lynch. It might also be noted that even with a very depleted team of experienced ministers the Taoiseach did nothing to reverse his demotion of Flanagan who was left in Lands.

Within the party Lynch resisted the attempt to force an emergency Ard-Fheis. He leant upon his majority in the parliamentary party as evidence of support, giving time to the new party managers to arrange the 1971 Ard-Fheis which provided him with an officer board and national party executive loyal to his policies. To see all this as a simple matter of manipulating party personnel, however, is to ignore the results of the double by-election in Donegal and Dublin County in December 1970 which showed a willingness by the voting public to accept the status quo without recourse to a general election. The findings of public opinion polls by Irish Marketing Surveys in 1970 also confirmed an overwhelming acceptance of Lynch's leadership.

Indeed the interim judgement on the cabinet crisis and Lynch's leadership must be to reinforce the general argument of this essay—to stress the institutional strength of the Taoiseach's role within the Irish system. It would be going too far to say that he is impregnable, but it is evident that the incumbent can easily be seen to be indispensable. The whole episode bears out Churchill's experienced and measured judgement:

> at the top there are great simplifications. An accepted leader has only to be sure of what it is best to do, or at least to have made up his mind about it. The loyalties which centre upon number one are enormous. If he trips, he must be sustained. If he makes mistakes, they must be covered. If he sleeps, he must not be wantonly disturbed.

81

7

The Role

This examination of five men in office has been inevitably selective and incomplete. It has ignored some significant aspects of Irish political leadership. The absence of any discussion of de Valera's drafting of the new Constitution, for example, or of his handling of the neutrality policy during the war distorts the picture and perhaps understates the extent of his personal dominance; similarly there is no mention of Liam Cosgrave's role as a consciously responsible Leader of the Opposition in Lynch's handling of his cabinet crisis. But the essential purpose of the essay has been to concentrate on the group relationship within the cabinet as the most revealing indicator of the extent and limits of the Taoiseach's influence; necessarily comment has been limited to topics and events illuminating this theme on which reliable information was available. Any conclusion drawn from this kind of data must be regarded as tentative and provisional.

Politically, the single transferable vote system of election has offered an opportunity to narrow the scope of executive influence or at least reduce its capacity to impose initiatives on a conservative society. Within the party structures local support and selection of candidates remains the norm. The record of Irish elections indicates a population unwilling to accord any substantial majority mandate, although ready to renew a mandate to an accustomed government in office. Given parliamentary representatives whose main concerns are local, even parochial, and parties sensitive to established community interests and values, the main restraints on executive policy-making spring less from the institutions of politics than from the value systems of the community. No other body in the society can compare in potential influence and power with the state machine; the cabinet still holds within itself a near-monopoly of major public decisions and, with rare exceptions, it is clear that what it decides will be accepted by the Oireachtas and implemented loyally by the public service. Within the cabinet no single actor—irrespective of office, experience, personality or power base—can compare in influence with the Taoiseach; what he says, with rare exceptions, will be listened to and what he wants achieved.

The situation stated in these terms seems classic for the exercise of strong, positive, even heroic leadership. The role seems designed for a chief. But the evidence of fifty years and five incumbents indicates that it is in the 'rare exceptions' mentioned above that one discerns the reason why successive Irish leaders have been forced to accept a chairman's role. When they have stepped beyond that, or attempted to alter the system—as, for example, in the two attempts to change the electoral machinery—they have been repudiated. Moreover, despite the concentration of power in their hands they have often failed to make their policy purposes operationally effective: Cosgrave could not convert the people to a willing acceptance of the Treaty, de Valera could not persuade them to a restoration of Irish, Lemass was unable to inaugurate a more rational system of labour relations. Change, whether in terms of negotiations with the North or of educational reform or of regional planning, is most successful when it is allowed to ripen into maturity; leaders can plant seeds, they must be careful not to force the growth and cannot expect an early harvest. Leadership in Ireland has become routinised; it operates within and through established procedures, it depends for success on an elaborate and inter-connected system of administration and control. Departures from the practices and conventions of collective cabinet responsibility are apt to strain the whole system. It is this which has fashioned the role of Taoiseach in Ireland.

The over-all performance of the five men who have held

office so far shows considerable variation in style but a remarkably close attachment to the chairman's role. Cosgrave set the pattern by eschewing an innovatory policy and establishing a role for the President within the Executive Council corresponding to that accorded to the Prime Minister in nineteenth-century Britain. The style and charisma of de Valera, as already suggested, has obscured the extent to which he, too, sought agreement before proceeding to action; he looked like a chief but performed as a chairman. Circumstances, previous experience and personal preference combined to curtail Costello's leadership but could not eradicate the power of office; he may have been only *primus inter pares* but he was *primus,* the focus for attention and decision. Lemass emerges as the first Irish head of government seeking to change and enlarge the role of Taoiseach; although far removed in style from the ideal type chief he did undoubtedly introduce a new concept of executive leadership and enterprise into the Irish governmental system. Lynch, a self-conscious chairman, has been in measure paying the price of attempting to restore the Taoiseach-cabinet relationship to its pre-Lemass character; he has also recognised the need to strengthen the office institutionally—both the extension of staff in the Government Information Bureau and the appointment of an expert economic adviser in the Department of the Taoiseach are indicators of a cautious willingness to assert greater control.

Caution and conservatism remain key-words. Indeed the extraordinary stability of Irish political institutions might well be attributed to the fact that successive heads of government have recognised and respected the fundamental values associated with authority in Ireland. Leaders must work within the political culture and national style of authority available to them and at this point, it might be argued, the comparisons made between Taoiseach and modern British Prime Ministers break down. A willingness to accept, even welcome, strong government has been one of the most marked features of British political culture; it has been accompanied by a clear differentiation between leaders and supporters. Thus, for example, Richard Rose can comment of the British system :

84

most national politicians come from socially atypical backgrounds. This factor distinguished them in dress, in speech accent, and in their everyday routine from the majority of the peripheral public. This is in accord with the norms of the political culture, which support deference to public-school manners and to unusual educational merit. Politicians are not expected to be 'of the people' or to mix readily with them; rather, they are there to exercise their judgment and give leadership.[1]

No such norm, values, expectations operate in Ireland.

Irish attitudes towards authority are more familiar and ambiguous. Legitimacy is readily acknowledged, though without undue deference, and the rhetoric of those in authority often implies a dominant influence that they clearly do not possess. Attitudes towards central secular authority swing from continuous demands for grants, services and special treatment for local needs to equally vociferous resistance to what is often seen as 'interference from Dublin'. There is a curiously casual treatment of office holders reflecting this ambiguity; their power is recognised by a steady stream of suppliants seeking assistance while any aloofness, even a human demand for privacy, is quickly criticised. Moreover in a small homogeneous community the interest in political leaders is easily translated into personal gossip that can have a reductive effect.

The need for leadership and the exercise of power is moderated by the demand that the leader should not deviate far from accepted values and that the impersonality of executive action be tempered by the needs of known individual cases. Partly these attributes reflect the rural character of Irish society, partly the experience of a people caught until the late nineteenth century between an *ancien régime* that retained privilege and a central government system that was remote and alien. Perhaps, most of all, they reflect the general characteristics of a stable representative system in a small state. The load of decision-making is small, the range of choices constantly curtailed by external forces and internal possibilities, the political expectations preserved at a low level. The danger in that situation is that stability can degenerate into stagnation, leadership confine itself to echoing inertia rather than asserting a voice for initiative. Ireland has needed chairmen Taoisigh in order to create stability for a new state; facing the renewed internal problem of national unification and the external challenge of Europe we may be reaching a time when a chief will appear crucial, or at least desirable. But before accepting this as a political cure-all, it is important to stress the extent to which the role of Taoiseach is defined and delimited by the values of Irish political culture. This should not be taken as implying some crude cultural determinism forcing the leader to act within rigidly set limits but as indicating the difficulties and dangers of deviating from established patterns :

culture is only the backdrop to leadership. It must not be confused with actual creative acts of leadership. Such acts are rare but crucial in a democracy.[2]

And they are not simply the prerogative of the chiefs; chairmen, too, can create new ideas and patterns. So long as they do this with reasonable competence, it seems safe to assume that the role of Taoiseach will not alter radically.

NOTES: The Role

[1]Richard Rose, *Politics in England*, London 1965, 105.
[2]Erwin C. Hargrove, in *Political Leadership in Industrialised Societies*, 219.

Note on Further Reading

References are given in footnotes to chapters but major works are given below.

There is an extensive annotated bibliography in Lewis J. Edinger, ed., *Political Leadership in Industrialised Societies*, New York 1967.

For the British Prime Minister see Anthony King, ed., *The British Prime Minister : a reader*, London 1969.

A revealing and influential account of the American presidency is Richard E. Neustadt, *Presidential Power : the politics of leadership*, New York 1962.

The standard work on Irish government is Basil Chubb, *The Government and Politics of Ireland*, Oxford 1970. Chapter 7 incorporates in large measure his earlier study *The Government : an introduction to the cabinet system in Ireland*.

See also M. Ó Muimhneacháin, *The Functions of the Department of the Taoiseach*, Dublin 1960.

Earl of Longford and T. P. O'Neill, *Eamon de Valera*, Dublin 1970.

John Whyte, *Church and State in Modern Ireland*, Dublin 1971.

List of Members of the Cabinet from 1922 onwards

THIRD DÁIL (9th SEPTEMBER 1922—9th AUGUST 1923)

FIRST EXECUTIVE COUNCIL

Minister	Name	Date of Appointment	Date of Termination
President and Minister for Finance	W. T. Cosgrave	6/12/1922	20/9/23 21/9/23
Vice-President and Minister for Home Affairs	Kevin O'Higgins	6/12/1922	21/9/1923
Minister for Education	Eoin MacNeill	6/12/1922	3/10/1923
Minister for Industry and Commerce	Jos. McGrath	6/12/1922	21/9/1923
Minister for Local Government	E. Blythe	6/12/1922	15/10/1923
Minister for Defence	R. Mulcahy	6/12/1922	21/9/1923
Minister for External Affairs	Desmond Fitzgerald	6/12/1922	21/9/1923

MINISTERS NOT MEMBERS OF EXECUTIVE COUNCIL

Minister for Agriculture	P. Hogan	14/12/1922	15/10/1923
Minister for Fisheries	Finian Lynch	14/12/1922	15/10/1923
Paymaster General	Jas. J. Walsh	14/12/1922	15/10/1923

PARLIAMENTARY SECRETARIES

To the Executive Council	Edmund J. Duggan	6/12/1922
To the President	Daniel McCarthy	6/12/1922

SECOND EXECUTIVE COUNCIL

Minister	Name	Date of Appointment	Date of Termination
President	W. T. Cosgrave	20/9/1923	23/6/1927
Vice-President and Home Affairs	K. O'Higgins	21/9/1923	23/6/1927
Finance	E. Blythe	21/9/1923	23/6/1927
Education	(a) E. MacNeill	3/10/1923	24/11/1925
	(b) J. M. O'Sullivan	28/1/1926	23/6/1927
Industry and Commerce	(a) Jos. McGrath	21/9/1923	7/3/1924
	(b) P. McGilligan	4/4/1924	23/6/1927
Defence	(a) R. Mulcahy	21/9/1923	19/3/1924
	(b) W. T. Cosgrave	20/3/1924	21/11/1924
	(c) P. Hughes	21/11/1924	23/6/1927
External Affairs	D. Fitzgerald	21/9/1923	23/6/1927

MINISTERS NOT MEMBERS OF EXECUTIVE COUNCIL

Agriculture	P. Hogan	15/10/1923	23/6/1927
Fisheries	F. Lynch	15/10/1923	23/6/1927
Local Government and Public Health	Jas. Burke	15/10/1923	23/6/1927
Posts & Telegraphs	Jas. J. Walsh	15/10/1923	23/6/1927

PARLIAMENTARY SECRETARIES

Parliamentary Secretary to	Name	Date of Appointment	Date of Termination
E. Council	E. Duggan	21/4/1924 (Re-appointed under Mins. & Secs. Act, 1924)	9/5/1926
President	(a) D. McCarthy	6/12/1922	31/3/1924
	(b) Jas. Dolan	19/6/1924	23/5/1927
Finance	(a) J. M. O'Sullivan	1/12/1924	27/1/1926
	(b) E. Duggan	10/5/1926	23/5/1927
Defence	G. Nicholls	15/1/1925	23/5/1927

FIFTH DÁIL (23rd JUNE 1927—25th AUGUST 1927)

THIRD EXECUTIVE COUNCIL

Minister	Name	Date of Appointment	Date of Termination
President	W. T. Cosgrave	23/6/1927	11/10/1927
Vice-President	(a) K. O'Higgins	23/6/1927	11/7/1927
	(b) E. Blythe	14/7/1927	12/10/1927
Justice and External Affairs	K. O'Higgins	23/6/1927	10/7/1927
Justice & External Affairs	W. T. Cosgrave	14/7/1927	12/10/1927
Finance	E. Blythe	23/6/1927	12/10/1927
Education	J. M. O'Sullivan	23/6/1927	12/10/1927
Defence	D. Fitzgerald	23/6/1927	12/10/1927
Industry & Commerce	P. McGilligan	23/6/1927	12/10/1927
Lands and Agriculture	P. Hogan	23/6/1927	12/10/1927
Fisheries	F. Lynch	23/6/1927	12/10/1927
Posts & Telegraphs	J. J. Walsh	23/6/1927	12/10/1927
Local Government and Public Health	R. Mulcahy	23/6/1927	12/10/1927

PARLIAMENTARY SECRETARIES

Parliamentary Secretary to	Name	Date of Appointment	Date of Termination
President and Defence	E. Duggan	24/6/1927	25/8/1927
	Reappointed	21/9/1927	11/10/1927
Finance	J. J. Burke	24/6/1927	25/8/1927
	Reappointed	21/9/1927	11/10/1927
Fisheries	M. Roddy	22/7/1927	25/8/1927
	Reappointed	21/9/1927	11/10/1927
Justice	Jas. Fitzgerald-Kenney	18/8/1927	25/8/1927
	Reappointed	21/9/1927	11/10/1927

90

FOURTH EXECUTIVE COUNCIL

Minister	Name	Date of Appointmnt	Date of Termination
President	W. T. Cosgrave	11/10/1927	3/4/1930
Vice-President and Finance	E. Blythe	12/10/1927	3/4/1930
Posts & Telegraphs	E. Blythe	12/10/1927	3/4/1930
Defence	D. Fitzgerald	12/10/1927	3/4/1930
Education	J. M. O'Sullivan	12/10/1927	3/4/1930
Industry & Commerce and External Affairs	P. McGilligan	12/10/1927	3/4/1930
Lands and Agriculture	P. Hogan	12/10/1927	3/4/1930
Fisheries	F. Lynch	12/10/1927	3/4/1930
Local Government and Public Health	R. Mulcahy	12/10/1927	3/4/1930
Justice	J. Fitzgerald-Kenney	12/10/1927	3/4/1930

PARLIAMENTARY SECRETARIES

Parliamentary Secretary to	Name	Date of Appointment	Date of Termination
President and Defence	E. Duggan	13/10/1927	3/4/1930
Finance	J. Burke	13/10/1927	3/4/1930
Posts and Telegraphs	M. R. Heffernan	13/10/1927	3/4/1930
Fisheries	M. Roddy	13/10/1927	3/4/1930
Industry and Commerce	J. N. Dolan	13/10/1927	3/4/1930

FIFTH EXECUTIVE COUNCIL

Minister	Name	Date of Appointment	Date of Termination
President	W. T. Cosgrave	3/4/1930	9/3/1932
Vice-President, Minister for Finance and Posts & Telegraphs	E. Blythe	3/4/1930	9/3/1932
Defence	D. Fitzgerald	3/4/1930	9/3/1932
Agriculture	P. Hogan	3/4/1930	9/3/1932
Lands and Fisheries	F. Lynch	3/4/1930	9/3/1932
Local Government and Public Health	R. Mulcahy	3/4/1930	9/3/1932
External Affairs and Industry & Commerce	P. McGilligan	3/4/1930	9/3/1932
Education	J. M. O'Sullivan	3/4/1930	9/3/1932
Justice	J. Fitzgerald-Kenney	3/4/1930	9/3/1932

PARLIAMENTARY SECRETARIES

Parliamentary Secretary to	Name	Date of Appointment	Date of Termination
President	E. Duggan	3/4/1930	29/1/1932
Defence	(Re-appointed to President only)	19/2/1932	9/3/1932
Finance	J. A. Burke Re-appointed	3/4/1930 19/2/1932	29/1/1932 9/3/1932
Posts & Telegraphs	M. R. Heffernan	3/4/1930	29/1/1932
Lands and Fisheries	M. Roddy	3/4/1930	29/1/1932
Industry & Commerce	J. N. Dolan	3/4/1930	29/1/1932

SIXTH EXECUTIVE COUNCIL

Minister	Name	Date of Appointment	Date of Termination
President and Minister External Affairs	E. de Valera	9/3/1932	8/2/1933
Vice-President, Minister Local Government and Public Health	S. T. O'Kelly	9/3/1932	8/2/1933
Lands and Fisheries	P. J. Ruttledge	9/3/1932	8/2/1933
Industry & Commerce	S. F. Lemass	9/3/1932	8/2/1933
Finance	S. MacEntee	9/3/1932	8/2/1933
Agriculture	Jas. Ryan	9/3/1932	8/2/1933
Defence	F. Aiken	9/3/1932	8/2/1933
Education	T. Derrig	9/3/1932	8/2/1933
Justice	J. Geoghegan	9/3/1932	8/2/1933
Posts & Telegraphs	J. Connolly	9/3/1932	8/2/1933

PARLIAMENTARY SECRETARIES

Parliamentary Secretary to	Name	Date of Appointment	Date of Termination
(a) President	G. Boland	10/3/1932	2/1/1932
(b) Defence	Re-appointed	28/1/1933	7/2/1933
Finance	H. V. Flinn	10/3/1932	2/1/1933
	Re-appointed	28/1/1933	7/2/1933
Local Government and Public Health	Dr. F. C. Ward	10/3/1932	2/1/1933
	Re-appointed	28/1/1933	7/2/1933
Lands and Fisheries	S. O'Grady	5/11/1932	2/1/1933
	Re-appointed	28/1/1933	7/2/1933

SEVENTH EXECUTIVE COUNCIL

Minister	Name	Date of Appointment	Date of Termination
President and Minister for External Affairs	E. de Valera	8/2/1933	21/7/1937
Vice-President and Minister for Local Government and Public Health	S. T. O'Kelly	8/2/1933	21/7/1937
Minister for Justice	P. J. Ruttledge	8/2/1933	21/7/1937
Minister for Industry and Commerce	S. F. Lemass	8/2/1933	21/7/1937
Minister for Finance	S. MacEntee	8/2/1933	21/7/1937
Minister for Agriculture	Jas. Ryan	8/2/1933	21/7/1937
Minister for Defence	F. Aiken	8/2/1933	21/7/1937
Minister for Education	T. Derrig	8/2/1933	21/7/1937
Minister for Lands and Fisheries	(a) J. Connolly (b) F. Aiken (c) G. Boland	8/2/1933 3/6/1936 11/11/1936	29/5/1936 11/11/1936 21/7/1937
Minister for Posts and Telegraphs	(a) G. Boland (b) O. Traynor	8/2/1933 11/11/1936	11/11/1936 21/7/1937

PARLIAMENTARY SECRETARIES

Parliamentary Secretary to	Name	Date of Appointment	Date of Termination
President and Minister for External Affairs	P. J. Little	8/2/1933	14/6/1937
Minister for Lands and Fisheries and Minister for Defence	S. O'Grady	11/11/1936	14/6/1937
Minister for Local Government and Public Health	Dr. F. C. Ward	8/2/1933	14/6/1937
Minister for Finance	H. V. Flinn	8/2/1933	14/6/1937
Minister for Defence	O. Traynor	3/6/1936	10/11/1936

EIGHTH EXECUTIVE COUNCIL AND FIRST GOVERNMENT

Minister	Name	Date of Appointment	Date of Termination
President and Minister for External Affairs	E. de Valera	21/7/1937	30/6/1938
Vice-President and Minister for Local Government and Public Health	S. T. O'Kelly	21/7/1937	30/6/1938
Minister for Justice	P. J. Ruttledge	21/7/1937	30/6/1938
Minister for Industry and Commerce	S. F. Lemass	21/7/1937	30/6/1938
Minister for Finance	S. MacEntee	21/7/1937	30/6/1938
Minister for Agriculture	Jas. Ryan	21/7/1937	30/6/1938
Minister for Defence	F. Aiken	21/7/1937	30/6/1938
Minister for Education	T. Derrig	21/7/1937	30/6/1938
Minister for Lands	G. Boland	21/7/1937	30/6/1938
Minister for Posts and Telegraphs	O. Traynor	21/7/1937	30/6/1938

PARLIAMENTARY SECRETARIES

Parliamentary Secretary to	Name	Date of Appointment	Date of Termination
President and Minister for External Affairs	P. J. Little	21/7/1937	27/5/1938
Minister for Lands and Defence	S. O'Grady	21/7/1937	27/5/1938
Minister for Local Government and Public Health	Dr. F. C. Ward	21/7/1937	27/5/1938
Minister for Finance	H. V. Flinn	21/7/1937	27/5/1938
Minister for Industry and Commerce	S. Moylan	21/7/1937	27/5/1938

SECOND GOVERNMENT

Minister	Name	Date of Appointment	Date of Termination
Taoiseach	E. de Valera	30/6/1938	See following page
Minister for External Affairs	E. de Valera	30/6/1938	See following page
Tánaiste and Minister for Local Government and Public Health	S. T. O'Kelly	30/6/1938 30/6/1938	See following page 8/9/1939
Minister for Justice	P. J. Ruttledge	30/6/1938	8/9/1939
Minister for Industry and Commerce	S. F. Lemass	30/6/1938	16/9/1939
Minister for Finance	S. MacEntee	30/6/1938	16/9/1939
Minister for Agriculture	Jas. Ryan	30/6/1938	See next page
Minister for Defence	F. Aiken	30/6/1938	8//91939
Minister for Education	T. Derrig	30/6/1938	8/9/1939
Minister for Lands	G. Boland	30/6/1938	8/9/1939
Minister for Posts and Telegraphs	O. Traynor	30/6/1938	8/9/1939

PARLIAMENTARY SECRETARIES

Parliamentary Secretary to	Name	Date of Appointment	Date of Termination
Taoiseach and Minister for External Affairs	P. J. Little	30/6/1938	26/9/1939
Minister for Local Government and Public Health	Dr. F. C. Ward	30/6/1938	See next page
Minister for Finance	H. V. Flinn	30/6/1938	See next page
Minister for Lands	S. O'Grady	30/6/1938	See next page
Minister for Defence	S. O'Grady	30/6/1938	28/8/1938
Minister for Industry and Commerce	S. Moylan	30/6/1938	28/8/1938

SECOND GOVERNMENT

(Re-organised Cabinet—European War, 1939)

Minister	Name	Date of Appointment	Date of Termination
Taoiseach and Minister for External Affairs	E. de Valera	30/6/1938	1/7/1943
		30/6/1938	2/7/1943
Tánaiste	S. T. Ó Ceallaigh	30/6/1938	2/7/1943
Minister for Local Government and Public Health	(a) P. J. Ruttledge	8/9/1939	14/8/1941
	(b) E. de Valera	15/8/1941	18/8/1941
	(c) S. MacEntee	18/8/1941	2/7/1943
Minister for Justice	G. Boland	8/9/1939	2/7/1943
Minister for Industry and Commerce	(a) S. MacEntee	16/9/1939	18/8/1941
	(b) S. Lemass	18/8/1941	2/7/1943
Minister for Finance	S. T. Ó Ceallaigh	16/9/1939	2/7/1943
Minister for Agriculture	Jas. Ryan	30/6/1938	2/7/1943
Minister for Defence	O. Traynor	8/9/1939	2/7/1943
Minister for Education	(a) S. T. Ó Ceallaigh	8/9/1939	27/9/1939
	(b) E. de Valera	27/9/1939	18/6/1940
	(c) T. Ó Deirg	18/6/1940	2/7/1943
Minister for Lands	T. Ó Deirg	8/9/1939	2/7/1943
Minister for Posts and Telegraphs	(a) T. Ó Deirg	8/9/1939	27/9/1939
	(b) P. J. Little	27/9/1939	2/7/1943
Co-Ordinator of Defensive Measures	F. Aiken	8/9/1939	2/7/1943
Minister for Supplies	S. F. Lemass	8/9/1939	2/7/1943

PARLIAMENTARY SECRETARIES

Parliamentary Secretary	Name	Date of Appointment	Date of Termination
Taoiseach and Minister for External Affairs	P. Smith	27/9/1939	26/6/1943
Minister for Local Government and Public Health	F. C. Ward	30/6/1938	26/6/1943
	H. V. Flinn	12/9/1941	26/1/1943
Minister for Finance	H. V. Flinn	12/9/1941	28/1/1943
	S. Moylan	10/2/1943	26/6/1943
Minister for Lands	S. O'Grady	12/9/1941	9/2/1943
	E. Kissane	10/2/1943	26/6/1943
Minister for Defence	S. Moylan	29/8/1939	26/6/1943
Minister for Industry and Commerce	S. Moylan	30/6/1938	9/2/1943
	S. O'Grady	10/2/1943	26/6/1943

THIRD GOVERNMENT

Minister	Name	Date of Appointment	Date of Termination
Taoiseach and Minister for External Affairs	E. de Valera	1/7/1943	9/6/1944
Tánaiste and Minister for Finance	S. T. Ó Ceallaigh	2/7/1943	9/6/1944
Minister for Industry and Commerce and Supplies	S. F. Lemass	2/7/1943	9/6/1944
Minister for Local Government and Public Health	S. MacEntee	2/7/1943	9/6/1944
Minister for Agriculture	Jas. Ryan	2/7/1943	9/6/1944
Minister for Education	T. Derrig	2/7/1943	9/6/1944
Minister for Justice	G. Boland	2/7/1943	9/6/1944
Minister for Defence	O. Traynor	2/7/1943	9/6/1944
Minister for Posts and Telegraphs	P. J. Little	2/7/1943	9/6/1944
Minister for Lands	S. Moylan	2/7/1943	9/6/1944
Co-Ordinator of Defensive Measures	F. Aiken	2/7/1943	9/6/1944

PARLIAMENTARY SECRETARIES

Parliamentary Secretary to	Name	Date of Appointment	Date of Termination
Taoiseach and Minister for Defence	E. Kissane	2/7/1943	7/6/1944
Minister for Finance	P. Smith	2/7/1943	7/6/1944
Minister for Industry and Commerce	S. O'Grady	2/7/1943	7/6/1944
Minister for Local Government and Public Health	Dr. F. C. Ward	2/7/1943	7/6/1944
	E. H. Childers	31/3/1944	7/6/1944

FOURTH GOVERNMENT

Minister	Name	Date of Appointment	Date of Termination
Taoiseach and Minister for External Affairs	E. de Valera	9/6/1944	18/2/1948
Tánaiste	(a) S. T. Ó Ceallaigh	9/6/1944	14/6/1945
	(b) S. F. Lemass	19/6/1945	18/2/1948
Minister for Finance	(a) S. T. Ó Ceallaigh	9/6/1944	14/6/1945
	(b) F. Aiken	19/6/1945	18/2/1948
Minister for Industry and Commerce and Supplies	S. F. Lemass	9/6/1944	18/2/1498
		9/6/1944	31/7/1945
Minister for Lcoal Government and Public Health	S. MacEntee	9/6/1944	18/2/1948
Minister for Agriculture	(a) Jas. Ryan	9/6/1944	21/1/1947
	(b) P. Smith	22/1/1947	18/2/1948
Minister for Education	T. Derrig	9/6/1944	18/2/1948
Minister for Justice	G. Boland	9/6/1944	18/2/1948
Minister for Defence	O. Traynor	9/6/1944	18/2/1948
Minister for Posts and Telegraphs	P. J. Little	9/6/1944	18/2/1948
Minister for Lands	J. Moylan	9/6/1944	18/2/1948
Co-Ordinator of Defensive Measures	F. Aiken	9/6/1944	19/6/1945
Minister for Health and Social Welfare	Dr. J. Ryan	22/1/1947	18/2/1948

PARLIAMENTARY SECRETARIES

Parliamentary Secretary to	Name	Date of Appointment	Date of Terminatio
Taoiseach and Minister for Defence	E. Kissane	9/6/1944	18/2/1948
Minister for Finance	P. Smith	9/4/1944	31/12/1946
	S. O'Grady	1/1/1947	18/2/1948
Minister for Industry and Commerce	S. O'Grady	9/6/1944	31/12/1946
Minister for Local Government and Public Health	Dr. F. C. Ward	9/6/1944	13/7/1946
	E. H. Childers	9/6/1944	21/1/1947
Minister for Local Government	E. H. Childers	22/1/1947	18/2/1948
Minister for Agriculture	P. Smith	1/1/1947	22/1/1947

H

FIFTH GOVERNMENT

Minister	Name	Date of Appointment	Date of Termination
Taoiseach	J. A. Costello	18/2/1948	13/6/1951
Tánaiste and Minister for Social Welfare	W. Norton	18/2/1948	14/6/1951
Minister for External Affairs	S. MacBride	18/2/1948	14/6/1951
Minister for Finance	P. McGilligan	18/2/1948	14/6/1951
Minister for Industry and Commerce	D. Morrissey	18/2/1948	14/6/1951
Minister for Local Government	T. J. Murphy	18/2/1948	29/4/1949
Minister for Health	N. C. Browne	18/2/1948	11/4/1951
Minister for Agriculture	J. M. Dillon	18/2/1948	14/6/1951
Minister for Education	R. Mulcahy	18/2/1948	14/6/1951
Minister for Justice	S. MacEoin	18/2/1948	7/3/1951
Minister for Defence	Dr. T. F. O'Higgins	18/2/1948	7/3/1951
Minister for Posts and Telegraphs	J. Everett	18/2/1948	14/6/1951
Minister for Lands	J. Blowick	18/2/1948	14/6/1951
Minister for Local Government	W. Norton M. Keyes	3/5/1949 11/5/1949	11/5/1949 14/6/1951
Minister for Industry and Commerce	Dr. T. F. O'Higgins	7/3/1951	14/6/1951
Minister for Justice	D. Morrissey	7/3/1951	14/6/1951
Minister for Defence	S. MacEoin	7/3/1951	14/6/1951
Minister for Health	J. A. Costello	12/4/1951	14/6/1951

PARLIAMENTARY SECRETARIES

Parliamentary Secretary to	Name	Date of Appointment	Date of Termination
Taoiseach and Minister for Industry and Commerce	L. Cosgrave	24/2/1948	13/6/1951
Minister for Finance	M. Donnellan	24/2/1948	13/6/1951
Minister for Local Goverment	B. Corish	24/2/1948	13/6/1951
Minister for Defence	B. Corish	27/2/1948	13/6/1951

SIXTH GOVERNMENT

Minister	Name	Date of Appointment	Date of Termination
Taoiseach	E. de Valera	13/6/1951	2/6/1954
Tánaiste and Minister for Industry and Commerce	S. F. Lemass	14/6/1951	2/6/1954
Minister for Finance	S. MacEntee	14/6/1951	2/6/1954
Minister for Health and Social Welfare	Jas. Ryan	14/6/1951	2/6/1954
Minister for External Affairs	F. Aiken	14/6/1951	2/6/1954
Minister for Lands	T. Derrig	14/6/1951	2/6/1954
Minister for Justice	G. Boland	14/6/1951	2/6/1954
Minister for Defence	O. Traynor	14/6/1951	2/6/1954
Minister for Education	S. Moylan	14/6/1951	2/6/1954
Minister for Local Government	P. Smith	14/6/1951	2/6/1954
Minister for Posts and Telegraphs	E. Childers	14/6/1951	2/6/1954
Minister for Agriculture	T. Walsh	14/6/1951	2/6/1954

PARLIAMENTARY SECRETARIES

Parliamentary Secretary to	Name	Date of Appointment	Date of Termination
The Government	J. Lynch	19/6/1951	2/6/1954
Taoiseach	D. O Briain	19/6/1951	2/6/1954
Minister for Defence	D. O Briain	19/6/1951	2/6/1954
Minister for Finance	P. Beegan	19/6/1951	2/6/1954
Minister for Social Welfare	M. J. Kennedy	19/6/1951	2/6/1954
Minister for Agriculture	G. Bartley	19/6/1951	2/6/1954
Minister for Lands	J. Lynch	5/11/1951	2/6/1954

SEVENTH GOVERNMENT

Minister	Name	Date of Appointment	Date of Termination
Taoiseach	J. A. Costello	2/6/1954	20/3/1957
Tánaiste and Minister for Industry and Commerce	W. Norton	2/6/1954	20/3/1957
Minister for Education	R. Mulcahy	2/6/1954	20/3/1957
Minister for Lands	J. Blowick	2/6/1954	20/3/1957
Minister for Justice	J. Everett	2/6/1954	20/3/1957
Minister for Agriculture	Jas. Dillon	2/6/1954	20/3/1957
Minister for Defence	Sean MacEoin	2/6/1954	20/3/1957
Minister for Posts and Telegraphs	Ml. Keyes	2/6/1954	20/3/1957
Minister for External Affairs	L. Cosgrave	2/6/1954	20/3/1957
Minister for Social Welfare	B. Corish	2/6/1954	20/3/1957
Minister for Finance	G. Sweetman	2/6/1954	20/3/1957
Minister for Local Government	P. O'Donnell	2/6/1954	20/3/1957
Minister for Health	T. F. O'Higgins	2/6/1954	20/3/1957
Minister for Gaeltacht	R. Mulcahy	2/7/1956	24/10/1956
Minister for Gaeltacht	P. J. Lindsay	24/10/1956	20/3/1957

PARLIAMENTARY SECRETARIES

Parliamentary Secretary to	Name	Date of Appointment	Date of Termination
The Government	J. O'Donovan	3/6/1954	12/2/1957
Taoiseach and Minister for Defence	D. J. O'Sullivan	3/6/1954	12/2/1957
Minister for Finance	M. Donnellan	3/6/1954	12/2/1957
Minister for Local Government	W. Davin	3/6/1954	1/3/1956
Minister for Agriculture	O. J. Flanagan	3/6/1954	12/2/1957
Minister for Industry and Commerce	P. J. Crotty	3/6/1954	12/2/1957
Minister for Local Government	D. Spring	16/3/1956	12/2/1957
Minister for Gaeltacht and Education	P. J. Lindsay	2/7/1956	24/10/1956

Minister	Name	Date of Appointment	Date of Termination
Taoiseach	E. de Valera	20/3/1957	23/6/1959
Tánaiste and Minister for Commerce	S. F. Lemass	20/3/1957	23/6/1959
Minister for Health	S. MacEntee	20/3/1957	23/6/1959
Minister for Finance	Jas. Ryan	20/3/1957	23/6/1959
Minister for External Affairs	F. Aiken	20/3/1957	23/6/1959
Minister for Agriculture	F. Aiken	20/3/1957	16/5/1957
Minister for Justice	O. Traynor	20/3/1957	24/6/1959
Minister for Local Government	P. Smith	20/3/1957	27/11/1957
Minister for Social Welfare	P. Smith	20/3/1957	27/11/1957
Minister for Lands	E. H. Childers	20/3/1957	24/6/1959
Minister for Education	J. Lynch	20/3/1957	24/6/1959
Minister for Gaeltacht	J. Lynch	20/3/1957	26/6/1957
Minister for Posts and Telegraphs	N. Blaney	20/3/1957	4/12/1957
Minister for Defence	K. Boland	20/3/1957	24/6/1959
Minister for Agriculture	S. Moylan	16/5/1957	16/11/1957
Minister for Gaeltacht	M. Moran	26/6/1957	24/6/1959
Minister for Agriculture	P. Smith	27/11/1957	24/6/1959
Minister for Social Welfare	S. MacEntee	27/11/1957	2/26/1959
Minister for Local Government	N. Blaney	27/11/1957	24/6/1959
Minister for Posts and Telegraphs	J. Ormonde	4/12/1957	24/6/1959
Minister for Agriculture	F. Aiken	20/11/1957	27/11/1957

PARLIAMENTARY SECRETARIES

Parliamentary Secretary	Name	Date of Appointment	Date of Termination
Taoiseach and Minister for Defence	D. Ó Briain	21/3/1957	23/6/1959
Minister for Finance	P. Beegan	21/3/1957	1/2/1958
Minister for Social Welfare	M. J. Kennedy	21/3/1957	23/6/1959
Minister for Industry and Commerce	G. Bartley	21/3/1957	24/2/1958
Minister for Finance	G. Bartley	24/2/1958	23/6/1959
Minister for Industry and Commerce	M. Hilliard	24/2/1958	23/6/1959

SIXTEENTH DÁIL (CONTD.)—(20th MARCH 1957—
15th SEPTEMBER 1961)

NINTH GOVERNMENT (23-24/6/1959—11-12/10/1961)

Minister	Name	Date of Appointment	Date of Termination
Taoiseach	S. F. Lemass	23/6/1959	11/1/1916
Tánaiste	S. MacEntee	24/6/1959	12/10/1961
Minister for Health	S. MacEntee	24/6/1959	12/10/1961
Minister for Social Welfare	S. MacEntee	24/6/1959	12/10/1961
Minister for Finance	Dr. J. Ryan	24/6/1959	12/10/1961
Minister for External Affairs	F. Aiken	24/6/1959	12/10/1961
Minister for Justice	O. Traynor	24/6/1959	12/10/1961
Minister for Agriculture	P. Smith	24/6/1959	12/10/1961
Minister for Lands	1. E. Childers 2. M. Moran	24/6/1959 23/7/1959	23/7/1959 12/10/1961
Minister for Industry and Commerce	J. Lynch	24/6/1959	12/10/1961
Minister for Local Government	N. Blaney	24/6/1959	12/10/1961
Minister for Defence	K. Boland	24/6/1959	12/10/1961
Minister for Gaeltacht	1. M. Moran 2. G. Bartley	24/6/1959 23/7/1959	23/7/1959 12/1/0/1961
Minister for Posts and Teelgraphs	M. Hilliard	24/6/1959	12/10/1961
Minister for Education	Dr. P. J. Hillery	24/6/1959	12/10/1961
Minister for Posts and Telegraphs	E. Childers	27/7/1959	12/10/1961

PARLIAMENTARY SECRETARIES

Parliamentary Secretary to	Name	Date of Appointment	Date of Termination
Taoiseach	D. Ó Briain	24/6/1959	15/9/1961
Minister for Defence	D. Ó Briain	24/6/1959	15/9/1961
Minister for Social Welfare	M. J. Kennedy	24/6/1959	15/9/1961
Minister for Finance	1. G. Bartley 2. J. Brennan	24/6/1959 27/7/1959	23/7/1959 15/9/1961
Minister for Justice	C. J. Haughey	9/5/1960	15/9/1961

104

TENTH GOVERNMENT (11-12/10/1961—21/4/1965)

Minister	Name	Date of Appointment	Date of Termination
Taoiseach	S. F. Lemass	11/10/1961	21/4/1965
Tánaiste and Minister for Health	S. MacEntee	12/10/1961	21/4/1965
Minister for Finance	Dr. J. Ryan	12/10/1961	21/4/1965
Minister for External Affairs	F. Aiken	12/10/1961	21/4/1965
Minister for Agriculture	P. Smith	12/10/1961	8/10/1964
Minister for Transport and Power	E. Childers	12/10/1961	21/4/1965
Minister for Industry and Commerce	J. Lynch	12/10/1961	21/4/1965
Minister for Local Government	N. T. Blaney	12/10/1961	21/4/1965
Minister for Social Welfare	K. Boland	12/10/1961	21/4/1965
Minister for Lands and Gaeltacht	M. Moran	12/10/1961	21/4/1965
Minister for Posts and Telegraphs	M. Hilliard	12/10/1961	21/4/1965
Minister for Education	P. J. Hillery	12/10/1961	21/4/1965
Minister for Defence	G. Bartley	12/10/1961	21/4/1965
Minister for Justice	C. J. Haughey	12/10/1961	8/10/1964
Minister for Justice	S. F. Lemass	8/10/1964	3/11/1964
Minister for Agriculture	C. J. Haughey	8/10/1964	21/4/1965
Minister for Justice	B. Lenihan	3/11/1964	21/4/1965

PARLIAMENTARY SECRETARIES

Parliamentary Secretary	Name	Date of Appointment	Date of Termination
Taoiseach	J. Brennan	12/10/1961	18/3/1965
Minister for Defence	J. Brennan	12/10/1961	18/3/1965
Minister for Finance	D. B. O'Malley	12/10/1961	18/3/1965
Minister for Lands	B. Lenihan	12/10/1961	21/10/1964
Minister for Justice	B. Lenihan	8/10/1964	2/11/1964
Minister for Lands	G. Colley	21/10/1964	18/3/1965

ELEVENTH GOVERNMENT (21/4/1965—10/11/1966)

Minister	Name	Date of Appointment	Date of Termination
Taoiseach	S. F. Lemass	21/4/1965	10/11/1966
Tánaiste and Minister for External Affairs	F. Aiken	21/4/1965	10/11/1966
Minister for Transport and Power	E. Childers	21/4/1965	10/11/1966
Minister for Finance	J. Lynch	21/4/1965	10/11/1966
Minister for Local Government	N. T. Blaney	21/4/1965	10/11/1966
Minister for Social Welfare	K. Boland	21/4/1965	10/11/1966
Minister for Lands and Gaeltacht	M. Moran	21/4/1965	10/11/1966
Minister for Defence	M. Hilliard	21/4/1965	10/11/1966
Minister for Industry and Commerce	P. J. Hillery	21/4/1965	13/7/1966
Minister for Agriculture	C. J. Haughey	21/4/1965	10/11/1966
Minister for Justice	B. Lenihan	21/4/1965	10/11/1966
Minister for Posts and Telegraphs	J. Brennan	21/4/1965	10/11/1966
Minister for Health	D. B. O'Malley	21/4/1965	13/7/1966
Minister for Education	G. Colley	21/4/1965	13/7/1966
Minister for Labour	P. J. Hillery	13/7/1966	10/11/1966
Minister for Education	D. B. O'Malley	13/7/1966	10/11/1966
Minister for Industry and Commerce	G. Colley	13/7/1966	10/11/1966
Minister for Health	S. Flanagan	13/7/1966	10/11/1966

PARLIAMENTARY SECRETARIES

Parliamentary Secretary to	Name	Date of Appointment	Date of Termination
Taoiseach and Minister for Defence	M. Carty	21/4/1965	10/11/1966
Minister for Industry and Commerce	S. Flanagan	21/4/1965	18/7/1966
Minister for Local Government	P. Brennan	21/4/1965	10/11/1966
Minister for Finance	J. Gibbons	21/4/1965	10/11/1966
Minister for Gaeltacht	P. Faulkner	21/4/1965	10/11/1966
Minister for Agriculture	P. J. Lalor	21/4/1965	10/11/1966

TWELFTH GOVERNMENT (10/11/1966—2/7/1969)

Minister	Name	Date of Appointment	Date of Termination
Taoiseach	J. Lynch	10/11/1966	2/7/1969
Minister for Education	J. Lynch	11/3/1968	27/3/1968
Tánaiste and Minister for External Affairs	F. Aiken	16/11/1966	2/7/1969
Minister for Transport and Power and Posts and Telegraphs	E. Childers	16/11/1966	2/7/1969
Minister for Agriculture and Fisheries	N. T. Blaney	16/11/1966	2/7/1969
Minister for Local Government	K. Boland	16/11/1966	2/7/1969
Minister for Lands and Gaeltacht	M. Moran	16/11/1966	27/3/1969
Minister for Justice	M. Moran	27/3/1968	2/7/1969
Minister for Defence	M. Hilliard	16/11/1966	2/7/1969
Minister for Labour	P. J. Hillery	16/11/1966	2/7/1969
Minister for Finance	C. J. Haughey	16/11/1966	2/7/1969
Minister for Justice	B. Lenihan	16/11/1966	27/3/1968
Minister for Education	B. Lenihan	27/3/1968	2/7/1969
Minister for Social Welfare	J. Brennan	16/11/1966	2/7/1969
Minister for Education	D. B. O'Malley	16/11/1966	10/3/1968
Minister for Industry and Commerce	G. Colley	16/11/1966	2/7/1969
Minister for Health	S. Flanagan	16/11/1966	2/7/1969
Minister for Lands and Gaeltacht	P. Faulkner	27/3/1968	2/7/1969

PARLIAMENTARY SECRETARIES

Parliamentary Secretary to	Name	Date of Appointment	Date of Termination
Taoiseach and Minister for Defence	M. Carty	16/11/1966	22/5/1969
Minister for Local Government	P. Brennan	16/11/1966	22/5/1969
Minister for Finance	J. Gibbons	16/11/1966	22/5/1969
Minister for Gaeltacht	P. Faulkner	16/11/1966	25/3/1968
Minister for Posts and Telegraphs and Transport and Power	P. J. Lalor	16/11/1966	22/5/1969
Minister for Agriculture and Fisheries	D. B. Davern	16/11/1966	2/11/1968

Minister	Name	Date of Appointment	Date of Termination
Taoiseach	J. Lynch	2/7/1969	
Tánaiste and Minister for Health	E. Childers	2/7/1969	
Minister for Agriculture and Fisheries	N. Blaney	2/7/1969	
Minister for Local Government and Social Welfare	K. Boland	2/7/1969	
Minister for Justice	M. Moran	2/7/1969	
Minister for External Affairs	P. J. Hillery	2/7/1969	
Minister for Finance	C. J. Haughey	2/7/1969	
Minister for Transport and Power	B. Lenihan	2/7/1969	
Minister for Labour	Jos. Brennan	2/7/1969	
Minister for Industry and Commerce and Gaeltacht	G. Colley	2/7/1969	
Minister for Lands	S. Flanagan	2/7/1969	
Minister for Education	P. Faulkner	2/7/1969	
Minister for Defence	J. M. Gibbons	2/7/1969	
Minister for Posts and Telegraphs	P. J. Lalor	2/7/1969	

PARLIAMENTARY SECRETARIES

Parliamentary Secretary to	Name	Date of Appointment	Date of Termination
Taoiseach and Minister for Defence	D. O'Malley	3/7/1969	
Minister for Local Government	P. Brennan	3/7/1969	
Minister for Social Welfare	J. Geoghegan	3/7/1969	
Minister for Finance	N. T. Lemass	3/7/1969	
Minister for Agriculture and Fisheries	G. Cronin	3/7/1969	
Minister for Education	R. Molloy	3/7/1969	
Minister for Industry and Commerce and Gaeltacht	G. Collins	3/7/1969	

Name		Effective Date
M. Ó Moráin	Resignation as Minister for Justice	5th May
N. T. Blaney	Termination of appointment as Minister for Agriculture and Fisheries	7th May
C. J. Haughey	Termination of appointment as Minister for Finance	7th May
K. Boland	Resignation as Minister for Local Government and Minister for Social Welfare	7th May
D. O'Malley	Appointed Member of Government and assigned Department of Justice	7th May
J. Brennan	Assigned Department of Social Welfare	9th May
G. Colley	Assigned Department of Finance	9th May
P. Lalor	Assigned Department of Industry and Commerce	9th May
J. Gibbons	Assigned Department of Agriculture and Fisheries	9th May
J. Cronin	Appointed Member of Government and assigned Department of Defence	9th May
G. Collins	Appointed Member of Government and assigned Department Posts and Telegraphs	9th May
R. Molloy	Appointed Member of Government and assigned Department of Local Government	9th May

PARLIAMENTARY SECRETARIES

Name		Effective Date
P. Brennan	Resigned as Parliamentary Secretary to Minister for Local Government	8th May
D. Andrews	Appointed Parliamentary Secretary to Taoiseach and Minister for Defence	8th May
M. Kitt	Appointed Parliamentary Secretary to Minister for Gaeltacht	9th May
L. Cunningham	Appointed Parliamentary Secretary to Minister for Local Government	9th May
M. O'Kennedy	Appointed Parliamentary Secretary to Minister for Education	9th May

CABINET SECRETARIAT 1922–

SECRETARY

Diarmuid O'Hegarty	16/1/22
John Power Moynihan	26/3/32
Maurice Moynihan	1/3/37
Nioclás S. Ó Nualláin	1/1/61

ASSISTANT SECRETARY

Michael McDunphy	30/1/22
Padraig Ó Cinnéide	29/12/37
Nioclás S. Ó Nualláin	22/1/47
Padraig Ó Loingsigh	July 1950–31/12/51
Charles H. Murray	1/12/53–6/9/59
Tadhg Ó Cearbhaill	1/1/61–13/7/66
Domhnaill Ó Suilleabháin	2/8/66–